Management in Islamic Countries

Management in Islamic Countries

Principles and Practice

UmmeSalma Mujtaba Husein

Management in Islamic Countries: Principles and Practice
Copyright © Business Expert Press, LLC, 2014.
All rights reserved. No part of this publication may be reproduced, stored in a retrieval system, or transmitted in any form or by any means—electronic, mechanical, photocopy, recording, or any other except for brief quotations, not to exceed 400 words, without the prior permission of the publisher.

First published in 2014 by
Business Expert Press, LLC
222 East 46th Street, New York, NY 10017
www.businessexpertpress.com

ISBN-13: 978-1-60649-674-9 (paperback)
ISBN-13: 978-1-60649-675-6 (e-book)

Business Expert Press International Business Collection

Collection ISSN: 1948-2752 (print)
Collection ISSN: 1948-2760 (electronic)

Cover and interior design by Exeter Premedia Services Private Ltd., Chennai, India

First edition: 2014

10 9 8 7 6 5 4 3 2 1

Printed in the United States of America.

Abstract

Islamic management is the interpretation of management practices as explicated in Islamic practices. The recent growth and interest in Islamic finance has led to researchers contemplating whether Islam offers an explanation with reference to various other areas in management studies. This book offers the Islamic perspectives on business ethics, marketing, leadership, and human resource management and explains to readers the tangible need of reading Islamic management.

In order to deliberate on any of the aforementioned topics the holy book, holy prophet, and other reliable scriptures are taken into account. This gives the reader a clear picture of how a given thought is originating and at the same time makes the book an authentic read.

For teachers, the book offers an easy explanatory text with models, exercises and examples, discussion questions, and study questions. For researchers references for extra readings are included. A geocentric manager can benefit from the text alike whilst reading with the aim of understanding management practices from an Islamic perspective.

Keywords

Islamic management, Islamic human resource management, Islamic leadership, Islamic marketing

Contents

List of Figures ix
List of Tables xi
Definition of Terms xiii
Introduction xv
Some Opening Pointers xvii

Chapter 1   Why the Need of Islamic Management Principles 1
Chapter 2   Business Ethics—The Islamic Perspective 11
Chapter 3   Marketing in Islam 33
Chapter 4   Human Resource Management in Islam 55
Chapter 5   The Islamic Perspective on Leadership 79

Appendix 99
Notes 101
References 105
Index 109

List of Figures

2.1	Relationship between legislation and business ethics in Islam	15
3.1	Relationship between need and want built-up—horizontal product development	36
3.2	Islamic product development process	37
3.3	Islamic marketing process	46
4.1	Starting self-progress	68
4.2	The need to change is linked to the need of knowledge acquisition	70
4.3	The knowledge acquisition process	71
4.4	The knowledge acquisition process and entities	75

List of Tables

2.1	Comparison of Islamic ethical perspective and the alternate ethical system	12
3.1	Using Islamic quotations to create promotional content	45
3.2	Decision making from different ethical perspectives	49
3.3	Class exercise on decision making in marketing from different ethical perspectives	49
3.4	Comparing marketing definitions	51
4.1	Human resource management—differences in perspectives	76

Definition of Terms

Pbuh (saww): peace be upon him (salutation and an expression of respect which Muslims use when names of any of the prophets are taken; in this text, Prophet Muhammad's name is pronounced).

SWT: Subhana watallah (an Arabic respect phrase used as a suffix when God's name is pronounced).

Holy Quran: Scriptures revealed to the Prophet Muhammad (pbuh).

Sunnah: Prophet Muhammad's way of life and his actions.

Hadith: Saying of Prophet Muhammad.

Citations from the Holy Quran are present in italics and the verse reference follows in brackets adjacent to the verse. At the end of the book, the reference list includes full citation of verses used from the Holy Quran.

Introduction

The connection between management theory and practice and religion is derived from the implications of religious writings. Authors deliberating on management with religious context generally consider their discussions within the framework of western/contemporary management, resulting in an intersection of the theoretical constructs of western management with the religious literature. This book does not put the reader at the crossroads of religion and management; instead, it assists readers in comprehending management from an Islamic perspective. I have shown the connection between business and religion by addressing management topics that transcend the realm of business yet encompass everything that a manager needs to act on in a general business environment. Therefore this book is not simply "another one"; readers will be able to see a marked distinction from the existing literature.

Islam offers a broad-based comprehensive system of business practices and perspectives. Within this text, both the newfangled notions from the Islamic viewpoint and comparison of these with western/contemporary management are presented.

Given the richness and complexity of religious traditions and literature, everything that is pertinent and said on a certain topic under discussion cannot be captured—both because there is wide literature available and because doing so is not the core focus. The spirit of using the sacred revelation, prophet's sayings, and other Islamic traditions has been to deduce the Islamic viewpoint in management for a certain theme under discussion.

To suit the needs of an organization wanting to modify its operations based on Islamic principles, my quest is to take into account the realities of life as a manager in a corporation. Therefore, situational practicality is discussed. As readers sift through the content, they will appreciate the rules offered within various facets of management such as leadership, marketing, human resources, and business ethics, making the book a complete guide to Islamic management (IM). Essentially, there is no one text that offers a wide range of management topics under one title in a concise form, which makes this book a new discourse that does not build upon previous editions.

Developing this book, I have kept in mind the various complexities an academic may face whilst delivering topics that are novel and when material available is in its formative years. This has led me to discuss the relevant topics in an appealing manner with a lot of extras bundled together. Further, time and again I have scrounged terminologies from the western/contemporary school of management so as to create amicable reading milieu for professionals, who want to understand how Islamic principles may differ or compare with the contemporary management. Being the first publication of its kind, it is designed not only to address the Islamic viewpoint in management, but the knowledge needs of educational institutions and polycentric and geocentric managers are also kept in mind.

This unpretentious endeavor, I hope, shall facilitate managers, academics, and researchers alike to comprehend principles of IM and the main differences between conventional and Islamic management. May God the Almighty accept this humble effort, accept it as a trivial endeavor in his path, and make it constructive for its readers.

Some Opening Pointers

Before the details of IM principles are discussed, it is prudent to enlighten readers on some points concerning fundamental principles that regulate the Islamic way of life. This shall enable the reader to grasp the knowledge that is further built using these fundamental principles. It is therefore a must read for those who want to gain the full value of the book.

What Is Islam?

Islam is a monotheistic religion, within which the primary belief is that the universe and all its entities are created by God. Muslims (followers of the religion Islam) believe in a sacred book "Quran" revealed by God to the messenger the holy prophet Mohammad (pbuh) in the form of verses. The Arabic version of the word God is Allah (SWT). In this text, we shall be using these interchangeably.

> The Islamic system of practice is derived from the Holy Quran, the sayings and actions of the holy prophet (Sunnah), and the interpretations derived by the learned scholars (Ulema) from these sources.

Sources of Islamic Law: Where Does Islamic Management Place Its Roots?

At this stage, it is astute to acquaint readers with the roots of IM. The Islamic system of practice is derived from the Holy Quran, the sayings and actions of the holy prophet (Sunnah), and the interpretations derived by the learned scholars (Ulema) from these sources. Obedience to the word of the holy prophet is emphasized in Quran as follows:

> *Say (O Muhammad), If you love Allah, then follow me; (if you do so) Allah will love you and forgive for you your sins.* (Quran 3: 31)

In the comprehensive system of life Islam offers, it does not only focus on spirituality of human beings, but it is also concerned equally with their social affairs, with a balanced approach. All human actions must always adhere to the boundaries prescribed through the noted holy book commands, prophet's conduct (Sunnah), and sayings known as hadith. His acts and deeds are authenticated by the Holy Quran in the following verse:

> *Nor does he (Muhammad) speak out of his desire. It is no less than revelation that is revealed.* (Quran 53: 3–4)

These teachings are all-encompassing and provide direction in every domain of life, whether social, economic, political, or religious. In Islam, it is the overall conduct of a human being that is imperative. Islam offers an all-inclusive system; in it, business relationships, employee and employer dealings, finance lending and borrowing, and premise for legitimate business are defined thoroughly. Islam expects a proper balance between profit-making and responsibility toward the society. For this purpose, the holy book "Quran" and the commands given by the divine revelations are to be followed.

In the preaching of Islam, all human beings are equal as children of Adam. Islam requires a human being to be able to follow the Islamic teachings that shall assist him in maintaining a balance between worldly desires and material things; this is because man is accountable to God for his deeds on the Day of Judgment. Thus, there exists a strong accountability system that makes man responsible for his actions.

Islam Prescribes a Human Being to Take Responsibility

Islam is a comprehensive divine religion that provides for a believer's (one who follows Islam) all needs and requisites encompassing their total lives. The ultimate aim in Islam is directed by belief in Allah (SWT); in practice, it entails total submission to the will of Allah (SWT)—the final authority. Being a complete system to follow, Islam bundles legislative rules, norms of living, dos and don'ts of earning a livelihood, marriage and divorce, raising children, and rules of heir and ownership to name a few, as a package that believers are to accept as they enter the premise of the religion. Following on the same lines, the necessity of commercial laws in Islam is quite straightforward; should Islam not supply its viewpoint, this would automatically imply the acceptance of all sorts of business operations; however, that is not the case. Islam offers very clear lines of reasoning and logic underlining the associated commercial premise whilst engaging in any sort of business.

> Islam is a comprehensive divine religion that provides for a believer's (one who follows Islam) all needs and requisites encompassing their total lives.

The principles from the Holy Quran and instructions provided by the holy prophet form a guide for Muslims to lead their lives. These prescriptions govern both family and business life and public and private affairs. The importance of work and earning a livelihood for oneself and providing for dependents is seen to be equivalent to acts of worship.

Importance of Trade in Islam

The Holy Quran directs Muslims to engage in trade:

God hath permitted trade and forbidden usury. (Quran 2: 275)

Following the instruction in the verse above, the Islamic view is that God has created this entire universe and has created the entities to facilitate and provide for human needs:

And He has subjected for you the night and day and the sun and moon, and the stars are subjected by His command. Indeed in that are signs for a people who reason. (Quran 16: 12)

The above verse is very encouraging as it accentuates the fact that the environment that God has provided is meant for human beings. They can use time (day and night), and the sun and the moon (light and energy) to their advantage. Certainly this lays onus on the human being, making him responsible for gaining benefit from the many entities in this world.

Similar acknowledgment and appreciation is seen in the religious book *NahjulBalagha*, which is a collection of sermons, letters, and sayings of Imam Ali (the fourth righteous caliph and the first Imam). The book has been translated into English under the title "Peak of Eloquence." In one of his letters written to the Governor of Egypt (pp. 329–330), the Imam wrote:

> Take good care of the merchants and artisans, and ensure their well-being whether they are settled or traveling, or working on their own. Those are the providers of benefits and goods, which they bring from far away by sea or by land through mountains and valleys, securing them for people who are unable to reach them. Those are the people who will assure you a durable peace and respected allegiance. Give them due care in your vicinity and in other areas of your land.

> According to the Islamic school of thought, businessmen or entrepreneurs are seen as providers of "benefits."

This is a very encouraging note as it explains the importance of merchandise in Islam. The entire business cycle is explained fairly well. Businessmen or entrepreneurs, as the Islamic school of thought terms them, are seen as providers of "benefits." It is important to note here that "goods" are not the "benefits" Imam Ali is referring to here. There is a much larger meaning to the gain that trade brought in at early times. Traders moving with goods from place to place were the only means to transfer knowledge and learn traits from far-flung areas. They were the cause of improvement in quality of life in their own local environment. Their learning would not only benefit one household but would spread to the whole community, and hence the benefit would mushroom in the entire community. Lewis (2005)[1] rightly points out here that, "Islam always encouraged trade and commerce as long as it is conducted within the framework of Holy Quran and the word of Allah as revealed to his prophet Muhammad (PBUH)."

> *The holy prophet[s] said: "There are seventy branches of worship, the best of which is earning a living lawfully."*[2]

Earning a livelihood is incumbent upon Muslims. One must comprehend this using the bigger picture, wherein the foremost undertaking of man in Islam is to serve God; however, in order to achieve this goal he needs to have sufficient food to survive, clothes to cover his body, and a place to live, as basic necessities. Thus providing for one's living and dependents is a requisite whilst fulfilling the larger aim.

> Islam has prescribed prayers for varied day-to-day concerns; among these, there are prayers for maintaining and increasing Rizq (sustenance).

As a matter of fact, this makes earning a livelihood a part of serving God and thus a form of worship.

Imam Sadiq (A.S.)[3] said to Umar Ibne Harith (a companion of the Imam):

> Don't leave acquisition of lawful sustenance, because it helps you in religion. Tether your camels and then rely on Allah.[4]

Role of Prayers in Islam and Prayers for Sustenance

In addition to the daily obligatory prayers that Muslims recite five times a day, it is common practice in Islam to have prescribed prayers for varied day-to-day concerns. For instance, there are *taqebat* (optional prayers that are recited after obligatory prayers), *Istisqa* (prayers for rain), prayers for healing and cure, and an expanded list can encompass various diurnal concerns. Islam attaches a great deal of importance to trade and business, and this is evident when one notices prayers prescribed for maintaining and increasing *Rizq* (sustenance). It is quoted from the Holy Quran:

> *And whoever is careful of (his duty to) Allah, He will make for him an outlet, and give him sustenance from whence he thinks not.* (Quran 65: 2–3)

When this verse was revealed, some companions of the prophet closed their doors and turned to worship only, saying: Our sustenance is assured. When this information reached the holy prophet (pbuh), he called them and asked: Why did you all do this? They said: Our sustenance is guaranteed. To which he responded: If anyone acts in this way, his needs will not be fulfilled. It is necessary for you to supplicate and work too.[5]

The question of work has a lot of importance for acquisition of sustenance. Hisham Saidalani says: Imam Sadiq (A.S.) said: "O Hisham! When you see that if two groups are fighting in the battlefield and it is time to fight, then on that day also, do not stop working for acquisition of sustenance."

Further, note a verse from the Holy Quran, quoted below, that encourages mankind to explore earth in which means and resources of one's living are pledged to be present. However, the keyword *fulfillment of one's life* is worth exploring as we launch the effort of understanding Islamic perspectives of business ethics.

> *It is We Who have placed you with authority on earth, and provided you therein with means for the fulfillment of your life: small are the thanks that ye give!* (Quran 7: 10)

> In Islam, the focus of all activities remains on the submission to the will of Allah (SWT) and any form of work as a source of income also falls under the umbrella connotation of spiritual elevation.

It is simple to note that in fulfilling the means of one's life, the forthright understanding is the endeavour for earning one's livelihood as discussed above; nevertheless, the focus in Islam is on both human beings' principal needs as well as their spiritual needs. Thus, there is a higher level of fulfillment, which is deemed to be the fundamental objective of a believer's life; it is to attain spiritual elevation. The section below discusses how commercial activity also forms a way and link that fosters religious devotion causing spiritual progress.

Business: More Than Commercial Activity in Islam

Since in Islam the focus of all activities remains on submission to the will of Allah (SWT), various ways of attaining spiritual elevation available to a believer, business, any form of work, or all as a source of income also fall under the umbrella connotation of spiritual elevation. Through following the set rules and regulations as suggested in Islam, that is, complying with the religion's premise, commercial activity can also be transformed into a means of increasing one's religious devotion, thereby not limiting business to a mode of earning funds to support one's life and dependents.

A different set of priorities, values, and principles drive business under the Islamic value system. To begin with, the principal difference between the said objectives of contemporary business and business as ought to be conducted from the Islamic lens is distinct; the primary

> Islam values the intention that human beings carry toward any sort of task be it for one's social or private life.

objective is not maximizing shareholder value, profits, or both. In fact, in conducting any trade, selling, production, dealing, venture, commercial transaction, or all, the aim is to achieve morality, attainable via abiding by the rules set by the Allah (SWT) and as taught by the Prophet (pbuh), exhibited in his sayings and his way of life. These guide the business ethics in Islam.

Would the debate above imply that in a business following the Islamic perspective, there is no capacity to increase earnings or amplify profits? Islam is not against profits; one can target profits so long as certain conditions as decreed within the principles of the religion are complied with, for example, the earnings are coming from a Halal (permissible) source of income, the obligatory acts of Zakat (taxation: given to the poor), and the dealings are practiced under Islamic laws.

Thus, the raison d'être for having a working knowledge of IM principles is its divergence from conventional management practices. To reiterate, the underlying principle of business in the conventional school of thought is "profit maximization," and organizations that do not have profits as a business motive are treated under the banner of a different entity, such as "charities, NGOs," and so forth. In the IM school of thought, the core objective of any action is the pleasure of Allah (meaning God) and a believer's actions are always guided by Allah's commandments. Now, that surely is a major contrast to begin with and affects the subsequent course of actions that we shall discuss as we progress.

The Role of Intention (Niyya) in Islam

The holy prophet (pbuh) has said:

> *Verily, the action is (judged) by the intention (behind it).*

The above hadith underlines the significance of intentions; the criterion for any action, whether material or spiritual, lies in the purpose behind it.

Hence a sincere intention is the one "for the sake of God only." The value of intention is showcased in the hadith quoted above.

Intention is so valuable that even if a person is unable to perform a good deed, God will reward him for he had intended to do. Thus, Islam values the intention that human beings carry toward any sort of task, be it for one's social or private life. As we shall deliberate management principles from the Islamic perspective, the importance associated with intentions in Islam is essential to be understood.

Management principles from the Islamic perspective are beneficial for varied groups. Discussions on these shall follow in the premise of the book, and the relevance and ramification of these in today's business environment shall be highlighted.

A Short Learning Check

Be Sure You Can

- Explain the sources of Islamic teachings.
- Describe how Islam prescribes a human being to take responsibility.
- Explain the significance of intention in Islam.
- Relate to the role of prayers and subsequently the sustenance prayers.

Study Questions

1. What is the major reason quoted in the text above that is the main cause of divergence between the Islamic and the western/contemporary school of thought?
2. According to Imam Ali, what is the significance of merchants and traders and why should governments attach significance to their welfare?

CHAPTER 1

Why the Need of Islamic Management Principles

Study Objectives

After reading this chapter, you should be able to understand the following:

1. Importance of work, business, and trade in Islam
2. Growing interest of management and religiosity as a topic of interest to various groups
3. Why managers need to know about Islamic management (IM) principles

In the world of publishing, the first few exchange of documents between the potential author and the publishers entails submitting a book proposal. I remember doing one for "Islamic Management Principles": the book in your hands right now. I thought it would be a good idea to let all readers know why my ideas on the importance of this topic interested Business Expert publishers.

The story began when I submitted my suggestions on a book that would address the IM concepts in detail from an academic perspective and provide a practical aspect from a manager's point of view as well. I had proposed that I shall do this not just by providing the concepts from an Islamic viewpoint; instead, I shall tackle the comparison to contemporary western concepts of management, thereby building scholarly material in the emerging field of Islamic perspectives to management studies.

My argument was built up from research that underlined that up until now, much of Islamic perspectives discussed and published center around understanding Islamic finance and banking.[1] To me, because Islam is an all rounded code of conduct that offers insight into all walks of life, why weren't publishers addressing IM; there definitely is a dearth of academic content on IM related to topics, other than Islamic finance. Having said this, I completely agree that Islamic finance is a practical application based field and the growth in Islamic banking and related Islamic finance products requires new text, models, equations, and more to be elaborated periodically.

Surely I am not an Islamic finance expert! Let us go reverse to take on from where I left; this book was written to fill the present gap (not sure, if gap is the word—vacuum explains it better!) in academic text representing IM theory and practice. The aim is to make available broad text so that it shall cover requirements of courses offered on IM in colleges and universities. It shall also be a good read for managers wanting to know about dealing in Islamic business environments from a management perspective. Just read my excitement in the paragraph below, the exact words I used to sell this to the publishers:

The book aims to provide integrated, authentic content from various distinct areas of Islamic management. "A one-stop shop" for researchers, course developers, students and managers like. This book may well be a point of reference to develop and publish scholarly material in Islamic management. The variety of models and comparisons in form of tables offer the much needed academic insight into Islamic management theory.

The deliberated topics in the text include Islamic ethics, marketing, leadership, and human resource management (HRM) from an Islamic perspective. Easy to understand examples and simplified Islamic literature shall be part of the text to test and enhance reader comprehension on the concepts. Did I overpromise or overdeliver? As you read through the text, you will become the judge.

Now that the text is in a presentable format, I once again seek to justify the need of this new text book. And I begin by answering an expected question: "why a text that explicates management from Islamic viewpoint."

Islamic Management Principles Follow Islamic Finance

So the most talked about component in the field of management from the Islamic perspective is Islamic finance. Dedicated journals publish cutting-edge research, regular and frequent text books, handbooks, and academic conferences, and the icing on this academic cake is "the chartered Islamic finance professional" qualification. Just to swiftly pass by readers' minds, this is not the only certification available for Islamic finance professionals. The market offers a number of such certifications in different interested segments curious in learning the Islamic principles.

Following the developments of Islamic finance as both an academic and practiced subject, various aspects of Islamic practices have attracted interest from academicians. Certainly Islamic marketing is a popular field of interest; ad hoc articles on Islamic business ethics (IBE) in esteemed journals grab the reader's attention and quench the thirst of researchers working in the field. However, by and large, the Islamic perspective on various management topics such as leadership, human resources (HR), quality management, services marketing, human resource management (HRM), and many others requires thorough deliberation. Hence the starting point to substantiate the need for a text book forms filling the gap between the necessity and lack of available literature on IM in the form of a text book.

I feel the second most crucial element is the growing interest of academics in novel topics such as management and spirituality, management and religiosity, and management from the perspectives of divine religions. It is not uncommon to find lively and functional, special interest groups at leading management academies such as Academy of Management, academic conferences, and special issues in journals and handbooks with chapter contributions from renowned researchers addressing the need of time in the form of original and creative research. Judaism, Christianity, and Islam form the three Abrahamic religions that are also termed divine religions. Thus, any literature that focuses on Islamic perspectives, in actuality adds to and, addresses the need of the growing interest in the relationship between management and the above listed topics. This is because, IM can be treated as both a sub-topic under management and spirituality and management and religiosity. Certainly in the

> The growing interest of academics in novel topics such as management and spirituality, management and religiosity, and management from the perspectives of divine religions is an important factor pointing toward the need of a text elaborating IM principles.

academic world, this also calls for fresh perspectives. Hence this text book fits the straightforward phenomenon of demand and supply.

Next we have the reasons that arise from the business environment. Although these are addressed below in detail, I would like to enlighten readers on the significance of these pointers by commencing discussion below in a step-by-step process.

Affluent Muslim Customers

Blanchard[2] in his CRS Report for Congress, prepared for members and committees of Congress has revealed recent figures of leading Islamic states: Kingdom of Saudi Arabia's exports to the United States stand at $47.5 billion (up from $31.4 billion in 2010 but below the 2008 figure of $54.8 billion) and U.S. exports to Saudi Arabia are estimated at $13.8 billion (up from $11.6 billion in 2010). These figures also back the argument presented by some authors[3, 4] who relate such impressive trade values to the need of understanding Islamic business norms and ethics. Their discourse lays out an important point to consider, that is, the representation of Muslim countries as affluent customers in the secular world implies that norms and practices associated with these rich customers should be understood. This could mean raising awareness of Islamic products, traditions, laws, and regulations pertaining to business practices.

The Staggering Growth of Islam as a Religion

The key statistics for local authority in England and Wales have released the 2011 census[5] indicating that the number of Muslims increased the most (from 3.0% to 4.8%). There were increases in the other main religious group categories as well. However, within a market this exacerbation simply implies that there are more Muslims in the market—to buy from, to sell to, to communicate with, to employ, and to be employed for. Using contemporary management (CM) terminology, the growth in numbers of Muslim consumers would mean increase in the size of market segments. The larger a market segment size, the more vigilant companies need to be in looking after the needs of these. Given the statistics above, the escalating numbers make Muslims a sizeable market within the U.K.

This makes it prudent for a conventional organization to familiarize itself with the IM principles in practice, so as to be able to understand both the market and the customer; their associated values and principles.

The Good Old: Globalization

We borrow terminology from western/contemporary management: globalization that has resulted in increased interaction of different religious values through crossing borders of products and manpower. This has given way to a new business environment that demands the market to understand its behavior. This is the Islamic business environment. Within this new business environment is a large Muslim populace that constitutes around 20% of the world population and like any community is very much part of the global market place. Interestingly, Muslims are not just inhabitants of Islamic states only; a recent survey shows that one-fifth or 300 million Muslims, of the world's Muslim population, live in countries where Islam is not the majority religion (The Pew Forum, 2009, p. 1). For instance, China is home to more Muslims than Syria, more Muslims live in Russia than Jordan and Libya combined, and India has the third largest population of Muslims worldwide (The Pew Forum, 2009, p. 1). The case would've been much simpler if Muslim populace concentration was only found in Islamic states, since this would mean the reigning bylaws are Islamic but because socialist and secular states would have business regulations that suit its own systems this is a unique situation. In countries other than Islamic states, organizations need guidance on how to accommodate the religious practices of employees.[6] This drives the understanding that the need to be aware of the underlying principles driving IM is unquestionable.

For Whom is This Book a Useful Read

The situation is further distinct since managers, academics, researchers, and the elements in the larger market continuously require resources to update their knowhow. Although it is not all that easy to find a standalone text on Islamic marketing or Islamic finance, such content is not scarce. As a matter of fact, what forms viable sources to read the book is the attraction toward single distinct topics within management such as Islamic marketing perspectives, HRM in Islam (I refrain from providing actual names of textbooks). The notion is that these commentaries tend to discuss a single subject such as marketing, HR, ethics, and so forth leaving behind the dearth of a solitary compound text that amalgamates the core topics in management and addresses these from a broad spectrum. Within western/contemporary management, these kinds of academic text books on management principles and concepts in management are easy to find and have regularly updated versions with newer and revised case studies. This text aims to fill the gap by providing Islamic perspectives on management themes covering general management areas such as management principles, HR, marketing, business ethics, and leadership from an Islamic viewpoint within one textbook.

The content of the text has been developed, keeping in mind the needs and requirements of a geocentric manager, a globalized firm, an academic, a fresh graduate, and an aspiring employee for international assignment wishing to be acquainted with the Islamic business environment.

Academics shall find the text gratifying because of the structure and examples. I have made use of simple language so that it's easier to assimilate the concepts. The subject matter is initiated keeping in mind the current usage of western/contemporary management terminologies; thus wherever relevant, the conventionally used terms are exercised to enhance the usefulness of the theme under discussion. References of select extra readings are provided at the end of each chapter for the enthusiasts longing for the extra bit. (I am convinced that academics, researchers, and students would love these reserves.)

For the HR managers who are either appointing new recruits or training existing staff for an Islamic business environment, the content provided is thorough and extensive. In it you will discover the bottom line and basics governing Islamic principles; now that, I deem is considerably meaningful for managers to appreciate. I use the technique

> The content of the text has been developed, keeping in mind the needs and requirements of a geocentric manager, a globalized firm, an academic, a fresh graduate, and an aspiring employee for international assignment wishing to be acquainted with the Islamic business environment.

of simple examples in different scenarios to develop the sensitivity and consideration the environment would demand. Most of the discussion is accompanied by a managerial implication, which I guarantee is a worthwhile read.

It's a refreshing read for those eager to voluntarily understand the mechanisms governing IM principles. Because the text is categorically divided into distinct topics, those interested in marketing principles can have a pleasant read to expand their doctrine and so forth.

Fundamental Difference Between Islamic and Western/Contemporary Management Schools

The most suitable means to help readers begin understanding the core philosophy of IM is to understand the fundamental operational difference between IM and western/contemporary management. Organizations in a western/contemporary management environment are operationally designed to have their larger objectives based on profit maximization. These are then broken down to specific goals for various departments and down to managerial objectives, all in line with the organizational objectives.

Contrary to this, the larger aim of an organization in an Islamic environment is not profit maximization, it is submission to the will of Allah, and this is further reflected down to managerial objectives as well. The IM principles operate to have human objectives in line with the will of Allah. By stretching the organizational objectives to be in line with the will/commandments of Allah, western/contemporary management can operate with IM principles as well. The example fits well with Islamic banking departments within conventional banks. In these banks, as part of the banking stream, functions redefine objectives to fit the IM principles and hence are able to offer Islamic products, although fundamentally all other operations remain working under the conventional system. Islamic management deals with the management of organizations from the perspective of the knowledge acquired from revealed and other Islamic sources of knowledge and results in applications compatible with Islamic beliefs and practices.[7]

Overview of This Book

This chapter shall address why managers need to know about IM principles. How can one see the connection between Islamic principles and management theory? Essentially the idea behind this chapter is to convince the reader on the value of the text.

Chapter 2 discusses the Islamic perspective on "Business ethics," an important read for managers who wish to understand the underlying principles of decision making in an Islamic system. Various concepts that govern "general ethics in Islam," which is the authoritative notion have been explicated.

Chapter 3 covers marketing in Islam. It makes for a very interesting and deep read that is geared toward helping the reader clear misconception associated with "general marketing and Islam." I have attempted to address core marketing concepts in an effort for readers to comprehend what product development, product awareness, and pricing mean in Islam.

Chapter 4 deals with the distinct theme, HRM in Islam. A unique concept of what training and development are when viewed from the Islamic lens is a wonderful section. The career progression models are very stimulating for both academics and training managers.

The much researched topic "Leadership" is expressed from the Islamic viewpoint in the last chapter of this text book. Leadership principles are derived from the life and sermons of the holy prophet (peace be upon him, in text referred to as pbuh), letters and sayings of the prophet's companion, and Caliph Imam Ali.

At the end of sections, you are likely to find small learning checks with study questions. Each chapter is summarized with discussion questions toward the end. Extra readings and lists of references shall assist those who wish to further dwell into either researching or practically applying the concepts.

Wish you a refreshing read.

Discussion Questions

1. How does growth of a particular target market impact on business environment? Within the same context, discuss the growth of the Islamic market and its subsequent impact globally.

2. Different journals publish research that addresses management and religiosity. Name at least two such journals and discuss their aims and how these benefit you in your current status as a student, academic practitioner, researcher, or management professional.
3. Make a list of the new terminologies learned in Chapter 1 and discuss these with your friends to see if everyone understands the precise meaning.

Suggestions for Further Reading

1. Weir, D. (2008). Islamic perspectives on management and organization: *International Journal of Islamic and Middle Eastern Finance and Management* *1*(1), 84–87.

CHAPTER 2

Business Ethics—The Islamic Perspective

The aim of this chapter titled "Ethics—The Islamic Perspective" is to present the ethical course of action for managers from an Islamic viewpoint. In the modern world, the western/contemporary school of thought presents various notions to cover business ethics that do not necessarily apply to values, morals, and ethics as expressed through the Islamic lens.

This chapter explores the need of IBE; it details why Islam addresses business ethics. We then take into account the law of permissibility and business in Islam, followed by deliberation on the Islamic ethical system that forms the core of ethics associated with any walk in life.

The reasons are constructed using specific verses from the Holy Quran that are linked to business and commercial ethics in particular. The text below shall utilize guidance from the Holy Quran—divine manuscript unveiled to the holy prophet Muhammad (pbuh)—the sayings of the holy prophet, known as *hadith*.

As humans engage in work, encountering ethical issues is not scarce. As emphasized in the introductory remarks of the textbook, I have utilized the comparison approach throughout the text to help readers understand the difference between the western/contemporary school and the Islamic school of thought unambiguously. The ethical system from an Islamic perspective is different in its very foundation from the western contemporary ethical system that does not take into account the role of religiosity in defining ethics.

In the case of business ethics, the alternative ethical systems such as utilitarian, cultural relativism, universalism, rights, and justice approach are always open to amendments and alteration. And decisions inferred for the same situation vary vastly based on different ethical systems. On the other hand, the Islamic ethical system is preset, determined, and well-defined based on derivations from the sources defined. The fundamental difference between Islamic ethical perspective and the alternate ethical system is elucidated in Table 2.1.

Table 2.1 Comparison of Islamic ethical perspective and the alternate ethical system

Ethical system	Meaning	Islamic ethical perspective
Utilitarian system	Calculates costs versus benefits, that is, an act is deemed morally correct and right if the net benefits over costs (greatest good) are greatest for the majority (greatest number).	Islam does not serve the interest or benefit of a specific subject involved; instead any dilemma is resolved using the set of rules from the Holy Quran, prophet's sayings, and Sunnah, and is not affected by the quantity of beneficiaries.
Individualism view of ethics	Fundamentally serves one's long-term self-interests.	If one's self-interests are aligned with Allah's commands, then this is the way a decision should be made; however, if it JUST serves one's own ego, this is certainly unacceptable.
Moral-rights view of ethics	Protects the fundamental rights of all people, for example, employees' rights, free speech, health and safety, and so forth.	The moral-rights view covers just a minor section of Islamic business ethics (IBE). Hence it can be treated as a component of IBE only so long as rights of the employees are those approved by the Islamic laws (the superset as defined in Figure 2.1).
Justice view of ethics	Fair and impartial treatment of people according to legal rules and standards.	Certainly fair and impartial treatment is a universal set of "right" behavior; however, the main concern is the set of legal rules. The benchmark set of standards needs to be the Islamic standards that should be the superset as referred to in the discussions below.

Discussion—The Way Forward

It is evident from the description provided in Table 2.1 that when viewed from the Islamic lens, none of the ethical perspectives are complete. As a matter of fact, the utilitarian approach reads incorrect.

The flaws in each of these may well be discussed as part of classroom exercise or roundtable discussion in an office meeting whilst setting the code of conduct. The deliberations can focus on the deficiencies and the overlap of the western/contemporary ethical approaches when compared with the Islamic ethical perspective.

Having touched upon the major ethical views found in the western/contemporary school of thought, I shall now enlighten readers on what are moral standards in Islam and how these are linked to the superseding and dominant law of permissibility.

Learning Check: Be Sure You Can

- List the sources used to construct IBE.
- Understand various ethics views associated with the western/contemporary school.

Study Questions

1. Which of the ethics views covers a minor section of IBE? And how can this be justified?
2. What is the justice view in ethics and the counter understanding of the Islamic ethics viewpoint on justice?

Moral Standards and the Law of Permissibility

Ethics is the discipline that examines one's moral standards or the moral standards of a society to evaluate their reasonableness and their implications for one's life. In Islam the **law of permissibility** defines moral standards, study of which is termed ethics. The understanding in Islam is founded on the simple ground of whether a certain act is allowable according to the legislations outlined. The initial stage of any commercial activity has to have clarity. This implies that the very concept of the business ought to be *Halal* business, and it must begin with commercial dealings to fall in line with the stated laws of religion. The business aim is that in order to "do good we must do it right; the permissible way." The "right" referred to here is *Halal* business, that is, permissible commercial activity and the "good" is meant to be revenues earned on it. This view is further explained with the help of a *hadith* below: read carefully as to what the call of Islam is on a non-permissible activity.

> *Prophet Muhammad (s.a.w.w.) said: "Allah has cursed the intoxicating drinks, he who squeezes it out (from grapes), he who plants (grapes, etc. for intoxicants), he who drinks it, he who serves it, he who sells it, he who buys it, he who earns from it, he who transports it and he to whom it is transported."* (Al-Majlisi, Biharu 'l-Anwaar, vol. 79, p. 126).

The above saying clarifies that the entire value chain of the business is non-permissible and no commercial activity is acceptable. Keeping the above *hadith* in mind, let us consider the following question; what should be a manager's call on having to decide whether production of an intoxicated drink should be moved to developing countries to take advantage of labor conditions and lesser wages; would this be unethical according to Islam?

> If the "law of permissibility" disapproves of an activity, then the entire value chain of the business is non-permissible and no commercial activity is acceptable for that particular action.

What should be the response; keeping the *hadith* (saying of the holy prophet) above in perspective, the question is null and void because the business itself is not allowed under the premise of the religion.

The First Step

The narration from the holy prophet provides a clear hallmark on the business elucidated above, clarifying that doing right is the first step toward being able to do well, thereby implying that being ethical in an unlawful or HARAM business is insensible and raising ethical questions in an unethical dealing is futile. Therefore Islamic legislation is mirrored

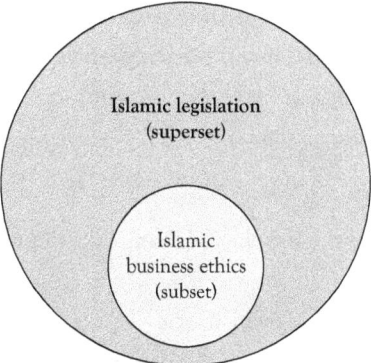

Figure 2.1 Relationship between legislation and business ethics in Islam

and shall always be reflected entirely in business ethics or simply said: IBE derives its elaboration from Islamic legislation. Perhaps, the best way of understanding the relationship is that there is total correspondence and 100% overlap between both as elucidated in Figure 2.1.

Islamic Business Ethics

We are now in a good position to define Islamic business ethics as follows.

Islamic business ethics (IBE) is the study of addressing business situations, activities, and decisions from Islam's permissibility perspective.

Ethical behavior in business from an Islamic perspective can be defined as "acts that are in line with the rules and standards of business practice as agreed upon by the Islamic school of thought."

Why Study Ethics in Business?

In the business world, decision making is a repetitive job. From initiation to the final verdict, the process involves series of assessments, evaluation, and finally the judgment. What consequences should a decision maker consider and rest the final outcome on? How should a situation be assessed?

In order to provide a reasonable answer and understanding on what drives the decision making from an Islamic viewpoint, it is prudent to study the salient components of the Islamic ethical system. As mentioned earlier, Islam is a complete legislative system and therefore the subject of business ethics in Islam is drawn from the umbrella Islamic ethical system.

Just as a quick reminder, readers may want to recall that Islamic laws are based on two main sources:

1. The Glorious Quran
2. The Teaching of the Prophet Muhammad (pbuh)

The latter is a combination of the "words," "deeds," and "endorsements" of the holy prophet. Further, the specific issues are handled by the legislation referred to as "*Shariah*."

An Important note that clarifies the stance of IBE and explains the disparity with the contemporary school of thought is explained in the section below.

Business Ethics in Islam Not an Oxymoron

In contemporary business, ethics is termed an oxymoron, which means that there is an inherent conflict between ethics and the self-interested pursuit of profit and that when ethics conflicts with profits, businesses always choose profits over ethics[1] because their principal objective is profit maximization. This is not encountered in Islamic perspective, since the aim here is not profit-making; there is never a situation of ethics conflicting with the business motive of augmenting profit. As a matter of fact, ethics and business sync jointly together as business ethics is a subset of the umbrella ethics that rules a believer's life.

> Within Islamic perspective, since the aim is not profit-making there is never a situation of ethics conflicting with the business motive of augmenting profit.

Pillars of Islamic Ethical System

The section below shall examine the mainstay of Islamic ethics by considering various key elements. These are first expressed in the primary terminology used in Arabic; its translation and further explanation are offered to provide an insight into how a particular concept is applied in the world of business. This explanation is offered in light of the text in Holy Quran and Prophet's sayings termed *hadith*.

Decision making at the workplace is often driven by situations that test our abilities to decide on the right thing to do. These can be a number of events, as serious as bioethics and medical ethics involving people's lives or the day-to-day operational issues encountered by employees; however, all require the concerned to carry out effective ethical action. Improper and erroneous choices are made as people start weighing multiple choices and selecting one under fear of losing their jobs, status, or benefits at their current employment. The Islamic belief system resolves the issue by offering the concept of "Tawakkal" explained below.

1. Tawakkal *Meaning Total Reliance, Belief, and Trust in ALLAH (SWT)*

> ...*and in Allah should the believers trust* (Quran 34: 122)

The literal meaning of the word *Tawakkal* has been derived from (*wakalat*), meaning "taking for oneself a representative," denoting that by faith and trust in Allah (SWT), a believer seeks to make Allah (SWT) his or her representative. What does this mean and how does it help? By placing one's trust in Allah (SWT), a believer adds to his or her limited strengths, the vast and all-encompassing power of the Creator. *Tawakkal* is a foundation stone in Islamic premise; by putting one's trust in the infinite power of Allah (SWT), the believer feels protected, and stays hopeful and positive.

> *Tawakkal* is a foundation stone in Islamic premise. By putting one's trust in the infinite power of Allah (SWT), the believer feels protected, and stays hopeful and positive.

How Does the Concept Apply in Business?

What is the sequential order of placing trust in Allah (SWT)? Does it mean one should reach any decision and then expect that trusting in Allah (SWT) would resolve matters for them without making the right judgment?

The Holy Quran in the verse (*ayah*) quoted below, emphasizes the order of trust.

> *Take counsel with them in the affair; so when you have decided, then place your trust in Allah; surely Allah loves those who trust.* (Quran 3: 159)

The above verse explains that in any matter of concern the first step is consultation with mates and fellowmen. Those from whom advice is sought consider various factors associated with the issue in order to approve a resolution, following which, a decision is pursued. After this decision-making process, the Holy Quran advises a believer ought to place his total trust in Allah (SWT).

In Islam, consultation is set as a way to exercise one's intellect; as the saying goes, two heads are better than one. It is narrated from Imam Ali that:

> *One who only follows his own opinion will perish, but one who consults people shares with them in their intellect.*[2]

In business and commercial dealing scenarios, more than often one starts relying on those who are placed in higher positions that are superior designations, such as one's boss, reporting authority, line manager, head of the department, and so forth. This invokes the thought process that other factors are influential enough to be a cause of incidents. Tawakkal is a concept that urges believers to understand that the best provision lies with the supreme authority as elucidated in the ayah below.

> *And Allâh is the Best of providers.* (Quran 62: 11)

Root of Ethical Dilemmas and Role of Tawakkal

The two triggers that cause decision makers to bring about immoral and erroneous judgments are fear of people and conditions. This consideration that one need not be influenced by the mighty and brawny because he or she knows and believes that Allah (SWT) is the supreme authority prevents any immoral decisions to be taken whilst facing ethical dilemmas.

Holy prophet said: "Whoever wishes to be the most powerful person among people must trust God."[3]

2. Taqwa (Piety)

The word "*Taqwa*" is derived from the root "*waqaya*" which means "to safeguard" or "to abstain." In Islamic terminology, it is defined as the action of restraining oneself from disobeying the commands of Allah (SWT). It relates to leading a virtuous life as discussed earlier. Running commercial dealings actually forms just a segment of one's life. Islam calls for a uniform approach; it does not desire believers to act entirely different at work settings and the reverse in their general conduct in lives. This implies that it also does not want believers to have different values from nine to five when they are engaged in earning a livelihood and switch to a different code of conduct when they end their day. Instead, it markedly expects a believer to have a general moral conduct extendable to ethical business demeanor that is based on Islamic teachings.

The desire to follow God's laws should lead people to value virtue, morality, and justice. All major religions contain moral tenets, and truly religious

> Islam expects a believer to have general moral conduct extendable to ethical business demeanor that is based on Islamic teachings.

people (i.e., those with an intrinsic orientation) should be less willing to engage in unethical behavior because they believe that God is omniscient and such behavior will be displeasing to Him.[4]

Thus if an individual is *Muttaqi* (one who follows Taqwa), this will inevitably reflect in his or her business dealings as well. Do recall from the note above that in Islam there is no difference between leading one's public and private life. The expected code of conduct (as explained below), which is the major tenets of Islam, shall result in ethical decisions within the business domain as well.

3. Honesty

O you who believe! Why do you say that which you do not do? It is most hateful to Allah that you should say that which you do not do. (Quran 61: 2–3)

Islam lays a great deal of emphasis on honesty. The above verse (*ayah*) condemns commitments that are just verbal and have no intention of reaching the practical stage. Islam wants followers to have their word and action to be the same. The expectation is that both the inward and outward personality must mirror each other. Knowingly giving one's word and not fulfilling it is abhorred.

In the life of the holy prophet (pbuh), one observes honesty at its apex; even before he announced prophethood, he was famously known as "*Sadiq*"—the honest. As a young man, he went on a trade expedition to Syria accompanying his uncle Abdulmuttalib. There, his honesty and reliability became so well known that he received the epithet of Muhammad, the trustworthy. Allah commands the believers in the Holy Quran on honesty as follows:

> *O you who believe! Stand out firmly for justice, as witnesses to Allah, even as against yourselves, or your parents, or your kin, and whether it be (against) rich or poor.* (Quran 4: 135)

I want to elaborate the above verse in relation to the specifics of business ethics and ethical decision making using the concept of whistle-blowing that surely is a much written about topic recently.[5, 6] Whistle-blowing is the decision of an employee to inform on illegal or unethical practices in the workplace. The call of Islam on this matter is unambiguous, if the above verse is considered. The most interesting part of the verse is that being a witness is regarded necessary even if it were against one's own self. This is the peak of honesty that Islamic values expect in circumstances that demand justice and a stand for the witness. Surely the whistle-blower fears revenge and retaliation that may come in different forms; however, the concept of "*taqwa*," that is, trust in Allah (SWT) comes into play in a situation like this. Certainly this also implies that a whistle-blower's intention should not be that of personal revenge against the wrongdoer.

We have well understood the role of intention in every action. If the intention is to punish the wrongdoer because of personal vengeance, then although the offender shall receive his due punishment, the whistle-blower would not have attained the desired status in the eyes of Allah (SWT) as he would've if his intention were solely based on reporting a wrong action because it is against the command of Islamic teachings.

Case Reading: Business and Honesty

Imran is a spice merchant in Pakistan. About 6 years back in 2006, he visited United Arab Emirates (UAE) for the first time and thought there was a huge market for dried whole and grounded spices from Pakistan, considering the local requirements and for re-export to European countries. Although his friends agreed, they candidly told him about traders' unpleasant experiences of dealing with a number of Pakistani importers. Imran could clearly gather that the situation at the offset showed a good need in the market and profits thereof; however, it did not favor the incumbent. Imran knew how to handle the situation. He obtained a trade license with a local partner (UAE laws require a local partner for business operations conducted within the city) and set up a shop in Deira's souk area, which is considered the spice trade market. To commence operations, he ordered spices from Pakistan and specifically asked sacks of 40 kg. The shipment was delivered and to his utter surprise the spices sack, expected to contain 40 kg, weighed maximum 37 kg! These were scheduled to be re-exported in half a day's time; his partners and workmen advised Imran to re-export as others do, since this was what he had received. Imran denied and asked for locally repackaging of the sacks and made sure that the consignment contained 40 kg/sack as per his commitment to the importing party. He continued the same exercise, initially bearing loss. Because of the high-quality supply and accurate weight delivered, orders started pouring in, putting Imran in a strong position to negotiate prices and select his suppliers from the home country accordingly. Because he was bringing in a large number of requisitions and concrete contracts, he soon became famous in Pakistan as an influential name in the spice export market. Four years down the line, he has one of the largest market shares, which is ever-growing.

4. Adl *(Justice)*

> *O ye who believe! Be ye staunch in justice, witnesses for Allah, even though it be against yourselves or (your) parents or (your) kindred, whether (the case be of) a rich man or a poor man, for Allah is nearer unto both (them ye are). So follow not passion lest ye lapse (from truth) and if ye lapse or fall away, then lo! Allah is ever Informed of what ye do.* (Quran 4: 135)

> The laws that encompass activities and conduct associated with permissible and forbidden behavior, concerning sellers, buyers, and any stakeholders in a commercial activity are all based on justice.

The entire Islamic economic system rests on the concept of (*Adl*) justice. The laws that encompass activities and conduct associated with permissible and forbidden behavior, concerning sellers, buyers, and any stakeholders in a commercial activity are all based on justice. Consider a scenario where an employee needs to inform authorities on the wrongdoings of one's employer, colleagues, subordinates, or all according to the Islamic viewpoint; the clear suggestion is in being just.

The situations could be diminutive problems such as excessive and forbidden use of Internet browsing, which is deemed to be a very common problem in the corporate world. USA Today reports how a number of companies are keeping an eye on workers' Internet use, or issues as substantial as the making of the Enron collapse.[7] The decision-making criteria rest on the balance of *Adl* (justice).

> *The Holy prophet (pbuh) said:* "*Even if the evidence goes against your own interest or against the interest of your parents or near relatives, it should not prompt you to alter the evidence or hide it.*"

It is gathered from the above how Islam encourages and wants believers to use their intellect and reason a situation such that it is aligned with the broad ethical system as explained above. It must be kept in mind that there exist specific rulings in the legislative system "*Sharia*" that guides a believer in precise and detailed issues. These can be asked and referred to from learned scholars; however, everyday concerns are resolvable, keeping in mind the basic ethical system.

Learning Check: Be Sure You Can

- Explain how law permissibility defines moral standards in Islam.
- Define Islamic business ethics.
- Reason why business ethics in Islam is not an oxymoron.

- Explain the pillars of the Islamic ethical system.
- Understand whistle-blowing in Islam.

Study Questions

1. What is the relationship between Islamic legislation and IBE?
2. With reference to business ethics when ethical decisions clash with the business motive, what kind of a situation arises?
3. How does the concept of Tawakkal apply to business?

Particulars of Business Ethics as Seen in Holy Quran, Sunnah, and Other Islamic texts

In addition to the basic elements in the ethical system, there are precise instances related to business practices that are explained in the religious text and content gathered below.

1. Importance of Prayer Timings and Business Dealings

Then when the (Jumu'ah) Salât (prayer) is finished, you may disperse through the land, and seek the Bounty of Allâh (by working, etc.), and remember Allâh much, that you may be successful. (Quran 62: 10)

From the verse above, it can be noted that from the Islamic perspective, the key to success is remembrance of Allah (SWT). Where this remembrance is possible at all times, the effort is further specified in the shape of five daily prayers and the Friday congregational prayers. A rather important aspect to observe is the significance associated with the Friday prayer and its timing, and the congregational prayer. In addition to the numerous benefits (that are out of scope for this particular text) it offers believers, we shall highlight the associated social benefits that show us the connection of how and why these are addressed in particular.

In congregational prayers, irrespective of class, color, and creed, believers stand together in rows to offer *Salah* (prayer). It promotes equality and is an economical way of bringing people together, offering a free networking

> In congregational prayers, irrespective of class, color, and creed, believers stand together in rows to offer *Salah* (prayer). It promotes equality and is an economical way of bringing people together, offering a free networking platform.

platform available to all attendees. The holy prophet (pbuh) said: the more the people present in congregational prayer, the more its reward, thus encouraging attendance in a gathering that can be of assistance in growing contacts, understanding people, and society's issues at large. The camouflaged reason to be present in congregations during prayers is quite evident from this discussion. However, not all can always reach places of worship; in that case, why give importance to prayer time and what is the relationship?[8] Imam Ali in his letter to Mohammad ibn-e-Abubakar, when he was appointed as the Governor of Egypt, wrote:

> *Offer your prayers on time, do not rush through them, and never delay in offering them. Remember that piety and nobleness of all your activities are subject to sincerity and punctuality of your prayers.*

The main highlight in the above extract is that nobleness, that is, graciousness and morality of all actions (that include businesses) depends on solemnity of prayers or, in other words, morality, virtue, and probity in business ethics, as business being part of our various activities is reliant on prayers offered. Therefore, we can see that there is a link established in Islamic teachings between business and prayers. The next aspect discussed below is pacts and their value in Islam.

2. Accords in Islam

> *Fulfil the covenant of Allah when ye have covenanted, and break not your oaths after the asseveration of them, and after ye have made Allah surety over you. Lo! Allah knoweth what ye do.* (Quran 16: 91)

> *And fulfill the promise; verily promise shall be questioned about* (Quran 17: 34).

This verse covers the individual agreements that are made amongst two parties. Islam believes in sanctity of covenant and obliges man to fulfill it without reservation; it makes no difference whether the one who has made the promise benefits from that covenant or is harmed by it once the pact has been made. It certainly is deemed to be an important virtue as mentioned in the Holy Quran. It has been mentioned as one of the distinct features of the faithful. The idea is that a society cannot fully realize its potential without the keeping of promises, that is, fulfillment.

> Islam believes in sanctity of covenant and obliges man to fulfill it without reservation.

The holy prophet (pbuh) said:

The person who has no covenant has no faith.[9]

This is a vital concern in the business world, where involved parties end up in ethical dilemmas pondering whether a deal made should be written off in favor of a new lucrative proposition. Business ethics in Islam clearly rejects the idea and recommends respecting the initial accord made.

Another feature briefly described below addresses the importance attached to weighing goods accurately.

3. Weighing As It Should Be

And give full measure when you measure out, and weigh with a true balance; this is fair and better in the end. (Quran 17: 35)

The issue of setting of scales and accurate measurement is quite linked to the discussion presented above on honesty, justice, and keeping one's word and accords. Weighing is linked to setting standards in the business scenario. Fair mercantile is grounded in the pact that a promised deal that involves measuring goods against a certain weight is gauged accurately. All material goods should be quantified on the set standards as agreed at the time of finalizing the deal.

Many a time, whilst a deal is being finalized, the agreement is made verbally only; the short account below enlightens Islam's call on contracts.

4. Ensuring Partnerships Don't Fail: Writing Down Agreements

O you who believe! Whenever you enter into deals with one another involving future obligations for a certain term, write it down. (Quran 2: 282)

In order to ensure clarity, Islam guides businesses to document all contracts. How does this help in a trade scenario? A written note can be turned into evidence; it can be referred back to in times of need, states of confusion, or both. The question still remains: how does it assist in any form of moral predicaments? The answer is that, to a large extent it helps in the prevention of considerable issues to arise in the first place and further ensures that in the case of setbacks that may surface, a written piece can save the decision maker loads of hassle. Consider a manager signing a deal for X amount of dollars for a consignment of scrap materials for a large recycling plant. As the shipment was dispatched from the source, the dollar price fell in the market, decreasing the price of the shipment by half! As the consignment arrives on the port, the manager is called to submit the required documentation so as to release the goods. What should the manager do? Should he pull out of the deal? The management may ask him to do so. If he does, it benefits his organization; logically, why should he now stick to his word (especially if it were verbal) …this is surely an ethical dilemma? A written accord, transferring the decision making to the writing in black and white, saves the manager.

Further Discussion on Ethical Dilemmas— The Rightness of the Decision

Ethical dilemmas are broadly defined as situations in which two or more values are in conflict. In order to understand the applied and pragmatic view of business ethics from an Islamic perspective, the section below shall take a look at decision making of generic functions in an organization. We have picked the HR and sales and purchase department to further enlighten readers on the Islamic perception associated with the common concerns arising within these divisions. HR is a feature of all forms of business, whether public or private and even charitable institutions.

Decision Making in Human Resources

A number of functions at the heart of HR, such as selection, recruitment, induction, appraisals, and promotions may report rising ethical issues. Ethical dilemmas may arise in the aforementioned processes such as ensuring fairness in allocation of pay and benefits, equal opportunities, and ensuring assessment measures are impartial in recruitment and performance measurement. A survey of over 1,000 U.S. personnel managers[10] found that the most common areas causing ethical concern were favoritism in hiring, training, and promotion; sexual harassment; inconsistent disciplinary measures; not maintaining confidentiality; sex discrimination in promotion and pay; and non-performance factors used in appraisals. How does a manager resolve a moral situation arising on any of the grounds referred to?

Let us have a look at the excerpt of a letter given to one of the governors sent to Egypt in the time of Imam Ali's caliphate, advising him how to treat men under his governance.

> *You should not treat good and bad people alike because in this way you will be discouraging good persons and at the same time emboldening the wicked to carry on their wickedness. Everyone should receive the treatment which his deeds make him deserve.* (Letter 53, Nahjul-Balagha)

The clear indication in the above saying is that treatment of employees rests on their performance, and not caste, color, creed, nationality, other criteria, or all. The premise of the saying above addresses the core of most of the issues associated with HR (these are mentioned at the beginning of this section). The main suggestion offered is that the treatment offered to one should be gauged on his or her actions. Further, rewards are essential to give confidence to the doer and further advance the good. Here "the good" is the person behind the occurrence. According to the Islamic ethical system, the absence of a reward system would result in demoralizing the good performer and encouraging the deficient to keep performing under standards. Thus, the underlying reason of a performance-based rewards system

> According to the Islamic ethical system, the absence of a reward system would result in demoralizing the good performer and encouraging the deficient to keep performing under standards.

is twofold; not only does it fairly pay off the doer, but also its absence, that is, the dearth of an accountability process backfires by encouraging the wrongdoers to persist in their actions and further demoralizes those who are moral and responsible in any given setting. From the contemporary school of thought, Steiner and Gilliland have reported that if applicants perceive selection tests to be both fair and possess face validity, they have a more positive attitude toward the organization and the selection procedures.[11]

Decision Making in Purchase and Sales

Both purchase and salespeople play an important role in any organization. They are crucial to all stakeholders and the success of all ventures alike. Salespeople also face conflicts; they are the ones who buy goods from the suppliers and promise customers products and services on behalf of the organization—they are the boundary spanners, operating outside the company representing them in the field.

Five Traits to Be Avoided As Narrated by the Holy Prophet

The holy prophet asks to be cautious and avoid the following. He who is in business and buys and sells things must avoid five traits; otherwise he should not buy or sell anything:

- Usury
- Taking oath
- Concealing the faults or defects of goods
- Praising it wrongly when selling it
- Finding faults in it when buying it [12](narrated by the holy prophet[13])

> He who is in business and buys and sells things must avoid five traits (otherwise, he should not buy or sell anything): usury, taking oath, concealing the faults or defects of goods, praising it wrongly when selling it, and finding faults in it when buying it.

The *hadith* above provides the IBE philosophy in a nutshell. Business processes within the sales and purchase department can be studied in light of the above, as it provides clarity by declaring the fundamentals associated with practices.

Usury

The prohibition of usury or charging interest on any lending is a part of every Islamic school of jurisprudence and is described fully under the topics of Islamic finance. We shall not attempt to go into details as it is out of scope of the ethics theme. Nevertheless, the practice is proscribed.

Taking Oath

Swearing needlessly is deemed improper, and use of written accords clearly, describing a deal comprehensively, is advised. This is handled in a previous section (Ensuring Partnerships Don't Fail: Writing Down Agreements).

It is very common for salespersons to be making sales whilst being pressurized in meeting targets. In doing so, he or she may wrongfully go into raptures over the product/service to be sold or a sales situation, where a consignment is defective or may be deficient in materials. The holy prophet has forbidden such acts. When the prophet was young and had yet not announced his prophethood, he went on a trade expedition to Syria with his uncle. Some of the crops he was carrying got soaked in rain. When he reached the market, the seasoned traders advised him to hodgepodge both the soaked and good-condition crop so as to be able to sell all off the goods. The prophet disagreed, and kept both separate; he decreased the prices of the soaked crop, selling it at a much lesser price than the fine quality undamaged crop, offering a choice to buyers and not concealing the state of the crops sold. This strategy of ethical selling was much appreciated by the buyers and all the crops got sold. It worked and the buyers were very happy too.

Islamic buying and selling require treating the buyer and seller honestly; the buyer is also not given the undue margin of finding faults in the product.

Learning Check: Be Sure You Can

- List the particulars of IBE.
- Explain the social benefits of congregational prayers that translate to business opportunities.
- Understand decision making in HR and purchase and sales from the Islamic perspective.

Study Questions

1. Sara is a new employee in your organization taking over the marketing manager position vacated recently. The advertisement agency claims a verbal agreement was made with them before she joined the organization; however, now she is the new person on board. The company is now calling for new quotations because prices have dropped for the same tasks as agreed with the particular advertisement agency. Help resolve the ethical dilemma from the Islamic perspective.
2. What do you understand from the following statement: "Islamic ethical system works on internal motivation?"

Summary

What is the foundation of IBE? It is through internal motivation. How can this be said? Through establishing a connection with the supreme authority, the business ethics practices from the Islamic viewpoint make it easy to follow the legal composition. The internal motivation works on creating a self-check system in place, easing the decision-making process and almost creating an ethical officer inside one's own decision-making system. That suggests a moral decision by weighing different options against the umbrella ethical system and suitably offering a reasonable resolution.

The Islamic perspective makes a human believe in internal locus of control, effective with a long-term focus. Meaning, it is one's actions that determine the future, and life events are not fixated and powered by the employers we work for. Further, because the focus is not just on this world, if an employee/employer, any decision maker, or both is honest, just, and fair, he or she would reap the benefits in life hereafter (*the Islamic concept of day of judgment—the day of resurrection*).

Thus business ethics in Islam teaches that obedience is to the authority of Allah (SWT) only; it is instrumental to gain His approval and appreciation, which is possible through following the set of guiding principles. As decision makers, the obligatory feeling should therefore be to look at the ethical principles of fairness, justice, and honesty as explained above for guidance.

Discussion Questions

1. What do you understand by the term "Islamic business ethics?"
2. How does being a Muttaqi (one who follows Taqwa) impact business dealings?
3. What are the five traits to be avoided as narrated by the holy prophet (pbuh) whilst buying and selling things?

Suggestions for Further Reading

1. Badawi, J. A. (2010). Islamic Business ethics. *Spiritual Goods: Faith Traditions and the Practice of Business*, 295–323.
2. Rice, G. (1999). Islamic ethics and the implications for business. *Journal of Business Ethics 18*(4), 345–358.

CHAPTER 3

Marketing in Islam

Introduction

In a weekly meeting with my director of research, we happened to reflect upon whether there is anything such as "Islamic marketing." Her argument started from the notion of wasteful expenditure/extravagance in Islam: "*Israf.*" She offered her explanation on how marketing today (which in essence is contemporary marketing) focuses on consumerism and "creating a want." The Webster's dictionary defines consumerism as "the concept that an ever-expanding consumption of goods is advantageous to the economy" which in Islam is "extravagance/Israf," and is highly rejected. Just therefore, if marketing is based on consumerism then much of what she said is fairly similar to how people perceive the existence of Islamic marketing as a concept. To a large extent, this could not be disagreed!

Just to explicate what my short yet impressive (she was surely impressed!) conversation with her was about, I completely agree with her viewpoint that if marketing activities are all about overindulgence of food, clothing, and luxury goods then it has no place in the Islamic system. However, this also makes understanding marketing from the Islamic perspective even more important. Islamic marketing is one of the management concepts where variation in disparity with contemporary marketing is much larger than many other concepts in management.

Now wait a minute, the predicament is not "marketing," it's consumerism. Islam has allowed the use of all comforts and conveniences of life, and does not ask anyone to give up any such things. The Holy Quran says:

> *Muhammad say: Who has forbidden the adornment of Allah which He has brought forth for His servants, and to use the good things of His providing? Say: These on the Day of Resurrection will be only for those who were faithful in the life of this world.* (Quran 7: 32)[1]

> The Islamic model of consumption is not influenced by consumerism; making consumption a goal has negative effects, and is in line with concepts like extravagance, wastage, and spoilage and has been considered objectionable from the Islamic viewpoint.

Following from the verse above, the deliberation shall produce clarity. It shows that Islam encourages a different pattern of consumption that is not in line with the consumption model influenced by consumerism. Seyedinia[2] concludes the same; he emphasizes that consumption on its own is not an objectionable phenomenon, and Islam too encourages Muslims to fulfill daily needs of their lives. However, consumerism and making consumption a goal has negative effects, and is in line with concepts like extravagance, wastage, and spoilage and has been considered objectionable from the Islamic viewpoint.

Islam notes wastage of food as a very important subject, in a multifaceted meaning. Hence both wastage and overconsumption are not only against the principles of economic fairness; these are repudiated because of their injurious effects on one's health. The Quran says:

Eat and drink but be not prodigal. (Quran 7: 31)

Therefore the interpretation is not that Islam asks believers to abstain from fine drinks and food; nonetheless, it does restrict overindulgence. At another place the Quran says:

O you who believe! Eat of the good things with which we have provided you, and give thanks to Allah. (Quran 2: 172)

Note: The above discussion shall suffice since both consumption and consumerism are multifaceted themes of discussion that are out of scope of our text.

Further analyzing the verse above, the keyword is "pure"; hence the starting point is "*Halal*," that is, abiding by the law of permissibility. If concepts are scrounged from contemporary marketing, then within the sphere of Islamic marketing "product" becomes the primary factor. The foremost rule is "permissible business delivering

> The starting point in Islamic marketing is "permissible business delivering allowable products."

allowable products," whereby accentuating that Halal is not merely a brand element; instead it is part of a belief system and moral code of conduct, integral to daily living.[3]

A Short Learning Check: Be Sure You Can

- Understand that Islamic marketing differs largely from western/contemporary marketing conceptually.
- Explain why Islam follows a different model of consumption.

Study Question

1. Explain how consumption in Islam is not influenced by consumerism?

Focus in Islamic Marketing

Although we've ruled out detailed discussions on consumerism, we still hold on to consumption, which is the objective of production. Production generates "product," which is essentially the main ingredient in Islamic marketing. We shall now attempt to understand the following:

1. What is the significant role of product in the Islamic marketing process?
2. How does it vary from the importance of product within contemporary marketing?
3. How is product the most significant element in Islamic marketing?

While the objective of production in contemporary marketing is influencing demand of wants, the "Halal" product in Islamic marketing cannot JUST be influenced by a mere want. Given the objections to extravagant spending in Islam ("*Israf*"), this should be fairly easy to understand. It may just be prudent at this stage to differentiate between need and want. Human needs are basic requirements, our survival kits. Wants are built upon these needs and are not mandatory for living; however

> The "Halal" product in Islamic marketing cannot JUST (simply) be influenced by a mere want.

they enhance living standards. For example, soap required to shower is part of one's needs and a perfumed soap can be categorized as a want. Also remember that needs are easier to define, although they do vary with age, gender, environment, beliefs, and a wide variety of other factors. Wants on the other hand can be ever-growing, and the relationship between need and want built-up is horizontal and is explained in Figure 3.1.

The figure explains how basic model of any product that addresses 'need' is converted into a wants product when add-ons are inserted that keep expanding the wants base but do not enhance the need satisfaction at all. Hence a product that is developing horizontally via add-ons is purely built on wants. Wants can be both functional and emotional. Therefore any product, as a resultant of horizontal growth, is built with the sole concentration on emotional wants, resulting in sellable materialistic aspects. So, for example, consider the classic case of horizontal development in the mobile industry that focuses just on a bigger display screen on a mobile phone, flashy covers, less weight, and superior pixel size as add-ons. An investment in a purely horizontally developed product is not a likeable buying behavior in Islam.

> The product, as a resultant of horizontal growth, is built with the sole concentration on emotional wants, resulting in sellable materialistic aspects.

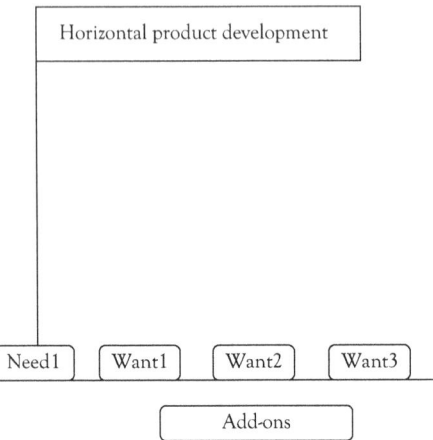

Figure 3.1 Relationship between need and want built-up—horizontal product development

Islamic Product Development Process

The essential principal in the Islamic product development process (see Figure 3.2) is that any add-ons must refine the "quality of the product" and at all times enhance the need satisfaction of the user. An enhanced product would mean better quality, which is reliant on research. If the product is electronic, then further research could mean better quality electric circuits used or improved health and safety standards; for a garment it may mean more durable material, tougher wear and tear, or both, and so on. In due course as needs improve because of the expansion in need base, for example, new segments arising such as new viruses discovered giving rise to a new segment of ailing populace, the product enhancement continues as a result of need refinement or need enhancement. However the preferred movement on product progression is always intended to be in the vertical and upward direction until the need is refined. So long as the product development is in the upward direction there is no restriction on accommodating add-ons from the horizontal axis of development

> The essential principal in the Islamic product development process is that any add-ons must refine the "quality of the product" and at all times enhance the need satisfaction of the user.

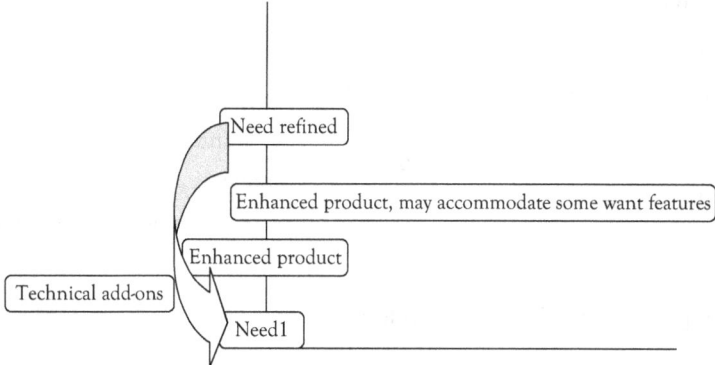

Figure 3.2 Islamic product development process

in the Islamic product development process. Nevertheless the focus of product development must always be on rightful need identification. This is based on the fact that human needs develop over a period of time. Who does not agree that basic needs have changed, and this is clear for the common man, who need not indulge in academic research, to a science researcher proving it through the use of lab instruments.

How Does Vertical Growth Occur?

> Vertical growth occurs only via scientific research followed by tangible development.

Undoubtedly vertical growth occurs only via scientific research followed by tangible development. Fundamentally, Islamic marketing bases its very foundations on academic research that identifies needs and develops products that are needs-based. This implies practicing "*justojo,*" that is, constant striving for the best way to slake the need. Hence the product development process in the Islamic marketing framework can be explained as follows:

Need refinement can be defined as follows:

The progression in human behavior that has happened from the ancient to the modern man, via research, or both to enhance the existing product that gratifies man's need better.

This is the area overlapping between contemporary and Islamic product development. Meaning, vertical growth can accommodate some aspects of horizontal wants and so long as the spotlight is not purely on the horizontal aspect of "wants," the product development can be considered as Islamic product development.

> Vertical growth can accommodate some aspects of horizontal wants and so long as the spotlight is not purely on the horizontal aspect of "wants," the product development can be considered as Islamic product development.

Steps in Islamic Product Development Process

1. Need identification
2. Devising the best possible method to slake the need

3. Research need refinement or need variation in diverse groups (example: need = food; groups—infants, toddlers, adolescence, adults, elderly, patients with special dietary requirements)

Need refinement could mean better infant formula being developed based on research, upcoming dietary requirements as a result of new ailments and syndromes. Hence, the second most important element associated with the product is "research and development (R&D)."

The example above explicates how the cycle is self-sufficient and ever expandable with the focus ultimately being "*justojo,*" that is, research that constantly works on identifying need refinement. The domino effect of product development as a result of need refinement is enhanced quality. What must not be disregarded in this process is creativity. Interestingly, advanced research can also encompass artistic quality. This is of the utmost importance in creating healthy competition. Look at the verse below from the Holy Quran:

O Children of Adam! Wear your beautiful apparel at every time and place of prayer; eat and drink, but waste not by excess, for Allah does not love those who waste. (Quran 7: 31)

In the above-mentioned verse, the use of an adjective such as "beautiful" shows the approval of creativity and the emphasis on "every time" and then specific mentioning of "place of prayer" stresses there is no time and space limit on use of good apparel. This may be a matter of independent debate nevertheless; we all agree beauty begins with cleanliness. Thus, even if one cannot commercially afford the most beautiful apparel, fine looking clothing that is clean is the expected attire Allah (SWT) commands human beings to be dressed in.

Both the above discussion and the concept of vertical product development signify the value of "product" in the Islamic marketing framework. Products that purely focus on "wants" do not adhere to Islamic principles, and hence are deemed inappropriate to the Islamic marketing function.

Note to remember: To reinforce, the prelude to the above discussion is that, criteria of a product to be "Halal."

Product Quality in Islamic Marketing

In discussing the above, the clear understanding is that an Islamic marketing framework is not just about the product. Instead it bundles "product quality" as an essential element of the product itself. And any substandard quality is deemed unacceptable. It is judicious to insinuate that quality also encompasses weight of the product, as mentioned in the Holy Quran:

Fill the measure when you measure and weigh with a right balance, that is proper and better in the end. (17: 35)

> The significance of accurate weight measurement does not just apply to a physical product; the time value and experience offered of service is just as important.

This verse implies the significance of weight not just for a physical product; the time value and experience offered of service is just as important. For example, a visit to a doctor should offer enough value of time to the ailing so that they come out satisfied and feel the experience of visiting the physician. Similarly, a lecturer in a classroom must use his or her time management skills so as to cover the content to be delivered and offer enough time to clarify any doubts that students may have.

Certainly, the value of the product/service is diametrically related to the price of the product and vice versa. The saying below, emphasizes the relationship that helps us seamlessly move to the next very influential component "pricing."

It is not allowed to change a price without altering the quality or quantity of the product because this is cheating the easygoing customer for illicit gain.[4]

Learning Check: Be Sure You Can

- Explain the significant role of product in the Islamic marketing process.
- Describe the Islamic product development process.
- Explain need refinement.
- Describe the "product quality" as an essential element of the product.

Study Question

1. You are in charge of the R&D team at a leading pharmaceutical company. A new study has identified the growing risk of diabetes in children under the age of 10. What kinds of add-ons are needed on the existing drugs to address the refined need?

The Rightful Price of a Product

Let me begin by offering personal experience just months back. I had the pleasure of visiting one of the Islamic tourist markets last summer, and was looking to secure lodging at a 4-star accommodation. We were unsuccessful in securing a booking at the preferred hotel. The place we wanted to stay had lots of tourist housing nearby. We were assuming that the newer version of the 4-star lodging we would now get hold of would cost us more. To our ultimate surprise, there was no price difference or premium pricing as we call it in the contemporary terminology on similar housing space. And the reason provided to us was that 4-star standards were met, but the newer services such as continental breakfast and varied massage services at the spa were all charged.

What a perfect example to explain that; pricing in Islam is all about charging a justified price coherent to the effort in material and labor required to produce the goods/service

> Pricing in Islam is all about charging a justified price coherent to the effort in material and labor required to produce the goods/service.

and not huge unjustifiable profits based on brand names, because the overall aim of the business is not "just profit maximization."

The justified price is nothing but "cost of the product + rational profit." This also means there is no harm in outsourcing production operations to cheaper locations. However, if this is practiced organizations can only charge "rational profit." This does not align well with the current practices of outsourcing to cheaper production locations with no impact on prices. As a matter of fact, this discounted manufacturing cost is used to escalate the profit margin. Readers can well appreciate the fact that from the western/ contemporary school of thought this is not an issue since the overall aim of business is number crunching. However, human rights groups for child labor, equal pay, and so forth see this as bad corporate behavior. To overcome such finger pointing, the western school of thought works out projects under the banner of corporate social responsibility. The Islamic pricing methodology, on the other hand, initiates operations with fair distribution of wages to workers (the first step in pricing the product is costs of production) followed by inputting this amount in the pricing equation to calculate the final price value of the product for the customer. Undoubtedly, the final price of the product needs to incorporate "all justifiable and accounted costs associated with production" and in the case of outsourcing, the material and final product movement cost needs to be accounted.

Then How Are Brands Formed?

Interestingly, in Islam, both pricing and branding are solely governed by the spot quality of the product. When Prophet Mohammad (pbuh) went on a trade expedition to Syria, heavy rainfall had half-spoiled some of the food commodities. As the trade market was being set up, traders started mixing the spoilt food with the intact merchandise. The holy prophet (pbuh) refused this action and instead instructed them to keep the two autonomously, and to be sold at different prices. The logic he offered was

> From the Islamic perspective, both pricing and branding are solely governed by the spot quality of the product.

1. one should not cheat the buyer by mixing differing levels of quality and selling it at a uniform price; and
2. offering choice to buyers who cannot afford first-grade quality due to financial constraints.

So, yes, this definitely proves that the brand and price difference is related to the quality of the product. And quality of a product is measured based on refined need or basic need, that is, on the vertical axis. This is contradictory to brand value in contemporary marketing, which is defined by the "add-ons" that are purely want-based, and in its premise brand exists in the mind of the beholder.[5] Within the western/contemporary marketing brand, knowledge is not the facts about the brand—it is all the thoughts, feelings, perceptions, images, experiences, and so on that become linked to the brand in the minds of consumers. The Islamic brand must offer real value to the consumer; it may then create decent yet truthful feelings toward the product, but, in all reality the value must be truly tangible. This is because truthfulness is unarguably a fundamental moral principle of Islam. To sum up and take the discussion forward, Islamic marketing is not about exaggerated mere wants or ballooned prices.

> The Islamic brand must offer real value to the consumer; it may then create decent yet truthful feelings toward the product, but, in all reality the value must be truly tangible.

Promotion

Contemporary marketing sees promotion as offering a key role in determining profitability and market success.[6] Academic studies quantify the net unit and net profit impact of promotions for a retailer and to understand the key correlates of this impact.[7] This points toward the function of promotion as related to profitability, in the marketing mix, as seen in the western school of management.

In terms of Islamic marketing, it is unethical for the salesman or customer relation advisor (CRA) to overpraise his products and attribute to them qualities which they do not possess.[8]

Having quoted the above, promotion is central to Islamic marketing as well and is deemed significantly imperative. However the scope of the role is much larger than just luring potential buyers by hook or by crook. Promotion in Islamic marketing is about creating rightful awareness of the product. The keyword remains "rightful"; that is, it completely rules out the false impression created by flashy packaging, mere celebrity endorsements to manipulate buyers, use of females without necessary covering, or couples involved in offensive acts. It rather should have a large forte. Not only should a promotion campaign be a means to provide for the best information regarding the product in a decent and appealing fashion, it should also educate potential buyers

> Promotion campaign should be a means to provide for the best information regarding the product in a decent and appealing fashion. It should also educate potential buyers on what need the product fulfills and how using a particular product is beneficial for the customer.

on what need the product fulfills and how using a particular product is beneficial for the customer. For example, advertisements for cleanliness products (whether body cleansing or home cleaning) should stress the importance of cleanliness as stressed within Islam such as in the following verse.

Truly Allah loves those who ask for forgiveness and strive to keep themselves clean. (Quran 2: 222)

The verses of Holy Quran and sayings of the holy prophet can be used by various product lines to enhance their promotional content. Use of verses from Holy Quran and the prophet's sayings can emphasize the importance of the "need" and therefore the product. On the whole, there is sufficient guidance available in the Islamic literature and sources in connection with health, hygiene, and nutrition and about the cleanliness of the air and the surrounding environment and other needs.

A few of them are quoted below and how the quotations can be used to create promotional content in line with Islamic marketing perspective. One of the columns (column 3) in Table 3.1 also analyzes the generic way promotional content is exhibited that contradicts the Islamic perspective.

As you must have gathered from the deliberations so far, Islamic marketing (see Figure 3.3) isn't about covetousness. It is about research followed by development, need refinement, quality product, justified pricing, and promotion strategies based on raising awareness pertinent to not only the product but the need the product is going to fulfill. There then seems to be a limited function that promotion can fulfill, but certainly that's not the case. As explained earlier, promotion is not intended to simply publicize the product, it is expected to make the consumer aware of the need. For example; the underdeveloped far-flung areas with populace having low literacy rates may not be aware of the importance of cleanliness personal hygiene, or both. In such a case, the role of product promotion in Islamic marketing is envisaged to raise awareness of the need and thus the product. Hence Islamic marketing is about disseminating information and creating a more conversant society where members of

MARKETING IN ISLAM   45

Table 3.1 Using Islamic quotations to create promotional content

Quote	Implication for promotion from Islamic perspective	Analysis—promotional content that contradicts the quotation	Instances of Islamic promotion using the quotation
Do not take food without having appetite and stop eating a little before the stomach is full.	The quotation addresses the need "food" and provides consumption guidelines.	Advertisements that urge people to * eat more for less; * eat as much as they can; * have double-sized, huge servings; are not in line with the Islamic quotation.	Our burger serves you nutrition—when you are hungry and does not bloat you to fullness because remember you must stop eating before your stomach is totally full. Through scientific research we have calculated the right serving size as per your age and height.
Use perfume and rub oil over your body and the hair of your head.	The quotation addresses a highly liked and recommended action "Mustahab."		Our range of products has oils suitable for body massage and hair massage.
Keep the compound and the front part of your house well swept and clean.	Islam not only stresses the need for personal hygiene, but it also emphasizes environment cleanliness.		The outsides need extra care—our products ensure your compound remains cleaner—longer.
Choose an open environment and a vast compound for living.	The quotation expresses choice for living space, and highlights that it should be spacious.	The need of housing for an ancient man was fulfilled by caves and the modern man can still live in cave space.	Our compound living is roomy and offers sizeable rooms. Choose the open environment you will enjoy to live in. Choose us.

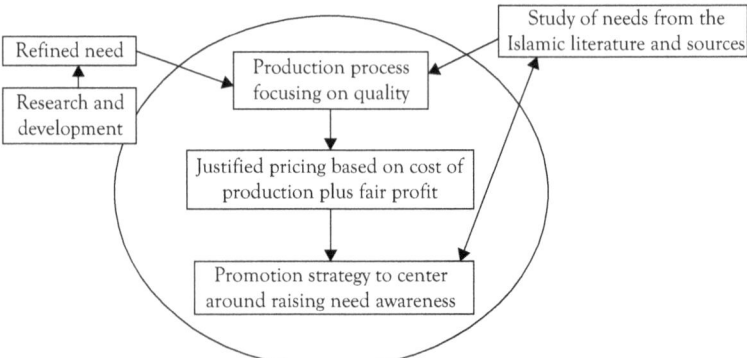

Figure 3.3 Islamic marketing process

the society understand their needs, the Islamic call on it, and a product that best satisfies the need.

Promotional Tools in Islamic Marketing

There could be many ways to achieve these goals of information diffusion. There is no limitation on whether the tech savvy cannot break down traditional thinking barriers and utilize tools such as the Web platform and social media. This implies that all progressive tools such as digital media and so forth can be deployed to make the end consumer aware of the product, so long as the use of these and any other tools is always exercised within the Islamic rules as specified above. What may serve as a reminder to readers here is that the law of permissibility defines the marketing function such that marketing campaigns for products other than "*Halal*" cannot be undertaken.

Putting things together from the above discussion, Islamic marketing heralds creating rightful awareness of a product/service that is permissible and fulfills the need of a consumer at all points and ensures that the fine line between need and a mere want is taken into consideration. It also ensures that the price the customer is paying for the product/service is well justified by the efforts that went into the production process plus a rational profit. Promotion in Islamic marketing takes on a larger role in the marketing mix as opposed to the space taken up by promotion in the contemporary marketing mix.

Learning Check: Be Sure You Can

- Describe the concept of "justified pricing."
- Explain need awareness through promotion strategies in Islamic marketing.
- Explain value of promotional tools in Islamic marketing mix.

Study Questions

1. How can guidance from the Islamic literature be used in developing promotional content?
2. What are the main differences between an "Islamic brand" and brand as explained in the western/contemporary marketing concept?
3. Discuss the statement, "Islamic pricing strategy initiates operations with fair distribution of wages to workers."

Throughout this chapter, I have been comparing and contrasting Islamic marketing with the western/contemporary marketing concepts. We have realized in due course that the overlap in concepts between both the schools of thought is fairly less. But, interestingly there is a concept in the marketing literature that seems to be either inspired from Islamic marketing or in terms of comparison can be visualized to have a fairly large overlap with how the concepts are placed in Islamic marketing. I am referring to "ethical marketing."

Ethical Marketing

Ethical marketing involves making marketing decisions that are morally correct and are driven by ethics that govern the organization. The idea is to encourage and uphold responsible and honest marketing. The concept does not only apply to fair advertising; it encompasses the entire marketing mix. The contemporary/western school of thought adopts ethical marketing because of various reasons, such as threats from ethical

> Ethical marketing involves making marketing decisions that are morally correct and are driven by ethics that govern the organization.

misconducts, pressure from environmental groups, legal standards, and various protection acts. Illegal behavior and non-adherence to dictated standards can result in negative publicity, scandals, and public embarrassment; these in turn mean huge costs to the company. Scandals and negative publicity can result in reduced share prices and stakeholder value. The image of the product in particular and corporate image in general can get tarnished. By practicing ethical marketing, organizations seek to develop competitive advantage. Organizations ask their marketing professionals to abide by governmental regulations, practice fair production and allow decent wages, say no to child labor, price the products carefully, remain transparent to consumers, treat them fairly, and ensure their privacy and keep it intact. Such practices help companies improve the brand image and retain loyal customers.

Let us examine the concept from the marketing perspective carefully. If marketing involves making decisions pertinent to product, pricing, and promotion (the three elements that are discussed in the core text), then ethical marketing means moral decisions on these three elements. If a situation arose within the marketing context, how would an organization resolve it? Clearly the answer is that the organization will utilize the ethical perspective that it generally does in any ethical dilemma within the business setting. There shan't be any difference between how contemporary marketing treats decision making in the marketing section and how it treats this in any other business sphere and situation.

It can base the decisions on universalism, just and moral approach, and the utilitarian view. The marketing decisions involving ethics may well include questions such as follows: Is the firm inflating the benefits of the product on its packaging? Is the firm charging profit margins that are not aligned with the reduced production costs? Certainly, the Islamic marketing perspective offers a clear response to each of these and many other questions that arise.

It would be beneficial for class discussion to consider each of these situations from all ethical perspectives. The best way is to take up role-play, where the situation is posed to students representing each ethical view. To provide a guide on how to proceed, samples are given in Tables 3.2 and 3.3 below.

Table 3.2 Decision making from different ethical perspectives

Situation	Ethical approach and decision	Ethical marketing and decision	Islamic marketing and decision
Should the firm charge profit margins that are not aligned with the reduced production costs?	Utilitarian approach: Calculates costs versus benefits, that is, an act is deemed morally correct and right if the net benefits over costs (greatest good) are greatest for the majority (greatest number). Decision: This is open to discussion; however, as observed outsourcing production is generally seen to reduce costs but does not result in reduced price.	Ethical marketing involves making a choice on rational and moral and socially responsible grounds. Decision: Honest price representation based on factual production costs should be decided as the product price.	An Islamic marketing decision on pricing will come from the understanding that a fair profit is charged on top of the production cost.
It is evident from the above analysis that ethical marketing decisions and Islamic marketing decisions are similar. Both the concepts assess and announce conclusions based on honest representation and keep social responsibility as a front when presenting a verdict.			

Group Exercise

Table 3.3 Class exercise on decision making in marketing from different ethical perspectives

Situation	Ethical approach and decision	Ethical marketing and decision	Islamic marketing and decision
Is it wrong to espouse advertisements that use selling techniques by focusing on vulnerable customers?	Individualism approach: Fundamentally serves one's long-term self-interests.		
Analysis:			

Ethical Marketing and Islamic Marketing—The Juxtaposition

What makes ethical marketing very similar to Islamic marketing perspective? Is it the stir that ethical marketing queries raise in the marketing process at an organization? Once there are fingers pointing and concerns are raised, decisions ought to be made. From the questions posed above, it is evident that these queries can arise from the production process through to pricing, promotion, and finally until the product reaches the end user. And if an organization chooses to practice ethical marketing, then the response is inevitably closer to the Islamic marketing response.

Selective Ethical Marketing

Many a time, organizations end up selecting areas within which the ramification of ethical marketing decisions shall be implemented, for example, production techniques, distribution channel or supplier selection, responsible advertising, treating workers fairly, and avoiding animal testing to name a few.

Undoubtedly in today's competitive business environment, the role of marketing cannot be underestimated and the Islamic business environment acknowledges and practices marketing as explained in the text above. The practices within the principles of Islamic marketing are similar to those observed by organizations undertaking ethical marketing. The decisions need to be in the Islamic framework that is governed by the law of permissibility and regulations as dictated by the Holy Quran and the holy prophet (pbuh). What is different between Islamic marketing and ethical marketing is that the contemporary school of thought assumes ethical marketing as seemingly a fix-up that assists an organization to develop a competitive advantage through selection strategy. However, in the Islamic marketing practice a decision needs to be thoroughly ethical; that is, if ethical means, as discussed, honest, factual, and socially responsible. This is because the principles within Islam gear humans toward submission to the will of Allah (SWT); hence Islamic marketing needs to remain focused throughout the

> In the Islamic marketing practice, a decision needs to be thoroughly ethical.

marketing process. The Holy Quran provides the guiding principle as follows:

> *Oh believers! Do not let your riches or your children divert you from the remembrance of Allah. If anyone acts this way, the loss is his own.* (Quran 62:9)

Comparing Marketing Definitions

At this stage, I would want to dissect the marketing definition as supplied by marketing news, in relation to the concepts discussed within the sphere of Islamic marketing. Do note that only sections of the definition that require further explanation have been elaborated. Table 3.4 is intended to brush up the concepts discussed so far, through the marketing definition provided below.

"Marketing is the activity, set of institutions, and processes for creating, communicating, delivering, and exchanging offerings that have value for customers, clients, partners, and society at large."[9]

A further comprehensive definition for Islamic marketing can be put together as follows:

"Marketing is the process of research and development that provides an output (product/service) which is a quality offering as a need satisfier, focuses on communication that raises need awareness, and has a value such that it brings human beings closer to Allah (SWT)."

Table 3.4 Comparing marketing definitions

Marketing news definition	Islamic perspective
Marketing is the activity	Marketing is the process of research and development
Creating offerings	Producing output as a need satisfier
Communicating	Communication that raises need awareness
Delivering and exchanging offerings	Delivering quality offerings
Value for customers, clients, partners, and society at large	Value for customers, clients, partners, and society such that brings human beings closer to Allah (SWT)

Summary

The discussion in the chapter highlights that the degree of variance between Islamic marketing concepts and western/contemporary marketing is much larger than in other management concepts such as HRM and so forth; the foremost being that Islamic marketing does not support the concept of consumerism, because fundamentally Islam is against overspending, "*Israf.*" This is evident in the likeable product development in Islam where add-ons should focus on quality rather than mere emotional features. That is, the Islamic product development process should be vertically inclined for a need until the need is refined due to new segments arising. Pricing in Islam must be justified based on the "cost of production." Promotion is central to Islamic marketing as it carries a much bigger aim than just appealing to and enticing potential customers. The key goal is to start at the very basic level of educating people on the various needs as explained in the Islamic literature.

Fairly large overlap is seen between ethical marketing concepts borrowed from western/contemporary marketing and Islamic marketing. The former school practices this due to pressure groups, whereas Islamic marketing operates ethically due to its very nature and prescription in its Islamic laws.

Discussion Questions

1. Given that Islamic teachings are against extravagant spending, how can you make a common man understand what is Islamic marketing?
2. What is need refinement and horizontal product development?
3. What is the fundamental difference between promotion in Islamic marketing and western school of thought?

Suggestions for Further Reading

1. Hassan, A., Chachi, A., & Latiff, S. A. (2008). Islamic marketing ethics and its impact on customer satisfaction in the Islamic banking industry. *Islamic Economics Journal 21*(1), 23–40.

2. Alserhan, B. A. (2010). On Islamic branding: brands as good deeds. *Journal of Islamic Marketing 1*(2), 101–106.
3. Zakaria, N., & Abdul-Talib, A. N. (2010). Applying Islamic market-oriented cultural model to sensitize strategies towards global customers, competitors, and environment. *Journal of Islamic Marketing 1*(1), 51–62.

CHAPTER 4

Human Resource Management in Islam

Analogous to the various topics in management, HR is a unique theme as it deals with living beings as opposed to marketing where the most significant subject is the "product/service" or business ethics where decision making in situations is the theme.

Contemporary management (CM) offers an array of theoretical constructs within HR. It is treated diversely through various schools of thought. These are the scientific, classical, behavioral perspectives of management. The scientific school of thought viewed a worker (human resource) simply as a means of increasing productivity and efficiency within a desired job. The rules and regulations in the scientific approach were very rigid and basically devised for a strict control on employees. These were geared toward maximum output, in other words profit maximization.

> Contemporary management offers an array of theoretical constructs within HR. These are the scientific, classical, behavioral perspectives of managements.

The move toward the behavioral perspective or human relations system is seen as a progress from the scientific system toward a more human-oriented system. The aim of scientific management was treating every task as a science wherein the employee was to understand the scientific way of working; however, the human relations school acknowledged that workers had individual needs. Under the banner of the human relations school, research commenced on concepts such as motivation at work, leadership, team work, and communication. The basic premise of study under human relations or the behavioral school as some scholars prefer to call it was the behavior of people working in groups. Nevertheless, the aim of both these schools was how to best get employees to perform to the best of their abilities only so that organizations could benefit the maximum in terms of profits. The popular term used then to manage employees was personnel management wherein the role of the personnel manager was to look after the employee's welfare at work.

Much later, the term human resource management replaced personnel management, and HRM was seen as "a strategic approach to managing employment relations which emphasizes that leveraging people's capabilities is critical in achieving competitive advantage"[1].

Why Islamic Human Resource Management?

Generally speaking, the role of religion in managing HR is considered under "the cultural aspect of managing workforce." Tayeb argues that in a predominantly Muslim country, Islam, through national culture, influences organizations.[2] Understanding the underlying philosophy of Islamic HRM is certainly practical in the growing multicultural and diverse workforces today. Such an understanding can help HRM practitioners reap benefits, should they be able to rise to the challenges posed by religion.[3]

In this regard, there has been very limited yet visible work existing in the literature addressing HRM from an Islamic lens. Most of the academic work has looked at the generic HR cycle that is scrounged from CM. The topics addressed encompass recruitment, training, appraisal, and other functions, all from an Islamic perspective. Islamic teachings offer relevant perspectives on HR issues as well.

The influence of Islam and its teachings on HRM, which are prevalent in certain countries, could be of interest to people and organizations that wish to do business with them, such as multinational organizations. It is very common for organizations in Islamic countries to have a prayer room and a norm to have a break for obligatory prayers, reduced working hours during the fasting month (Muslims fast in the ninth lunar month—Ramadan), and national holidays coinciding with religious commemorations and feasts. This is because in most Islamic countries, social, religious, and cultural factors are taken into consideration whilst devising policies. Therefore if a

> The influence of Islam and its teachings on HRM could be of interest to multinational organizations.

multinational company is operating in an Islamic state with geocentric or polycentric staffing strategy, it needs to adhere to the customary requirements. These practices are fairly common, thanks to globalization. Many service providers are seen catering to the needs of their external customers, for example, many western universities and international airports provide for a multi-faith room to cater to the needs of international students and travelers.

Organizations that operate with an Islamic perspective take into consideration the Islamic prescriptions that view the interests of employees and employers as complementary. Workers are treated as the creators of value in the marketplace and by necessity the primary force for economic growth and prosperity.[4] This accentuates the value of HRM as a function in the Islamic school of thought. Although the western school of thought has now pinned strategy to HR, this has generated the new term "strategic human resource management" wherein due to the resource-based view which points to the sources of HR advantage in building organizational capability, the human element is seen as a source of competitive advantage and subsequently success for an organization. The resource-based dimension of management portrays individual employees as investments rather than costs. Cost minimization was a phenomenon rooted in personnel management leading to the categorization of employees as one of the "aggregate commodities" that had to be managed in an organization.[5]

Thus the development of HRM in the western school of thought has come quite far and has been through various development phases. However, it must be clarified at this stage that within the contemporary school of thought, in its very essence, the HR functions have consistently been challenged to fight for its place.[6,7] The claim can be explained because even firms that generally spend huge amounts on training and reward structures, cut back on HR expenditures as the first resort when they face monetary setbacks or financial issues.

Learning Check: Be Sure You Can

- Discuss the different arrays of schools within the western concepts of HRM.
- Describe the importance of HRM from an Islamic perspective.

Study Questions

1. Under what category is the role of religion treated in western/contemporary management?
2. What can be the various reasons that HRM functions have fought for a place?

Core Principles in Islam Reflecting Implications for HRM

To assess the Islamic viewpoint on managing workforce, it is worthwhile to look at the core principles governing personnel relations and tasks in Islam. Management is all about decision making, and "locus of control" is one of the many factors that affect decision making. Locus of control can be simply explained as the extent to which an individual believes that he or she influences the outcomes of events in their lives (internal) as opposed to the influence of forces such as chance or fate (external). The internally focused individuals shall look inward for direction and often take the initiative while the externally focused count on the outside factors, such as the company owners, line managers, or company rules and tend to be compliant.[8, 9] People with a belief in internal control are more likely to change their behavior following a positive or negative reinforcement, than people with a belief in external control. However, for behavior change to occur, the reinforcement must be of value to the person.[10] The Islamic perspective of HRM has its foundations set in the teachings of the Holy Quran and Prophet's Sunnah and, in light of the studies mentioned, I pick the internal locus of control as a successful parameter in management decision making. In this regard, the Holy Quran elucidates the basis and formation of the internal locus of control via the verse below:

Everyone is entangled in the outcome of his deeds. (Quran 74: 38)

This literally implies that one is answerable for one's own actions, thereby stressing the fact that our actions are controlled by us because we are accountable for these.

From the western/contemporary school of thought, control mechanism is via sets of code of conduct, policies, and procedures devised by the organization, which literally provide workers with the framework of responsibilities (we are considering the HR functions) and they must abide by these rules. These sets of responsibilities are then controlled by an external force—the line manager. Thus the tenet of control is external; from a trivial action such as arriving to work on time to fulfilling the duties, the reigns of supervision are under the command of a manager. The verse above elucidates that the Islamic perspective instructs a different description. The belief in Allah (SWT) as the authority to whom man is answerable, emphasizes that one is responsible for one's own actions. Hence the onus of an action's outcome according to the Islamic viewpoint is on the one taking the action. This is a large demarcation in the HR perspective between the two schools of thought. And truly a large one, because the discussion points toward a reasonable deduction, that is, within the Islamic viewpoint the driving force behind human motivation is intrinsic motivation and that the western/contemporary school of thought runs on extrinsic motivation practices.

> In the Islamic school of thought, the belief in Allah (SWT) as the authority to whom man is answerable, emphasizes that one is responsible for one's own actions and hence control is internal.

Imam Ali, in Nahjul-Balagha[11] stated,

Persist in your action with a noble end in mind.... Failure to perfect your work while you are sure of the reward is injustice to yourself.

The Islamic belief system nails down the accountability concept in its basic tenets and the saying above accentuates the work ethics from the worker's end, in a simple expression: persistence, that is, continuous striving. The Islamic stance is very modest and clear-cut. If an employee is certain of the remuneration, incentive, or both, and yet fails to perform (the understanding is that the worker agrees on a sum, now knows what the work entails, and agrees to execute the assigned task) he or she is actually doing wrong to himself or herself by not continuously striving to deliver to the best of his or her abilities. This statement is worthy of note. From

> From the Islamic perspective, if an employee does not carry out his duties as agreed upon, it is he who loses out in the end, because the end is well-defined, thanks to the accountability concept.

the Islamic perspective if an employee does not carry out his duties as agreed upon, it is he who loses out in the end, because the end is well-defined, thanks to the accountability concept. This is simply because the employee is liable to Allah (SWT), if the organization is providing the promised sum, and the employee is blamed for laxity. He must realize that by being lazy or arriving late or not giving the required time to work, that is, by any means, by not performing to his fullest potential he is afflicting damage to himself thereafter. It is thus expected from a worker to produce hard work and exertion in the way of earning is seen as a source that washes away one's sins, as emphasized in one of the sayings of the holy prophet:

> Whoever goes to bed exhausted because of hard work, he has thereby caused his sins to be absolved.[12] (cited in Abdul-Rauf, 1984, p. 10).

Thus essentially from an Islamic point of view, the topmost layer of worker's motivation is intrinsic, that is, the individual's accountability to Allah.

In many ways, this is the key contrast between HRM practices in western/contemporary and Islamic management. In the contemporary school of thought, managing a workforce requires external "locus of control." The absence of a single, standard approach of managing the workforce insinuates disparity in rules in various organizations, different sets of codes of practices, rules and regulations, and accountability measures across organizations, even within the same sector. Many a time, there could be an impressive range of codes, rules and standards, and so forth set by talented HR directors; nevertheless, the success of these policies is totally reliant on how far these are adhered to by the employees and controlled by the supervisors.

If I were to create CM as the reference point, the readers can grasp the differences and realize the overlap between the CM and the IM perspective on HR. The "locus of control" factor sets HR practices in CM and IM poles apart and can have a variety of implications from the organization's perspective.

> The "locus of control" factor sets HR practices in contemporary and Islamic management poles apart.

An incident emphasizing how intrinsic motivation should guide the decision maker When two young boys brought in samples of different writings for judging and came to Imam Hasan (son of Imam Ali, and grandson of the holy prophet [pbuh]) for a decision, this was not treated as a simple and ordinary decision.[13] Imam Ali advised his son Imam Hasan to pay attention to the decision as "whatever decision you make you will be answerable before the Divine Justice on the Day of Judgment."

Managerial Implication

The managerial implication of being just amongst employees whether it be for the slightest effort and the largest competition, in actuality, arises from the internal drivers of accountability that lie at the heart of Islamic tenets. The growing inferences on such operational standard would mean correct appraisals, resulting in offering justified promotions. All these lie in line with the core Islamic principles.

Step 1

- Organization: Clarifies the reward/remuneration structure.
- Employee: Be just to own self by performing to perfection.

Learning Check: Be Sure You Can

- Distinguish between the internally driven "locus of control" in Islamic perspective to externally supervised in the western/contemporary school of thought.
- Explain how the above impacts decision making.

Study Question

What insights come from the accountability concept, present in the Islamic HR perspective?

As discussed earlier, most studies treat Islamic HR practices by dissecting the HR functions and studying these in light of Islamic teachings and principles. Before practicing the common methodology of running the HR functions through the Islamic lens, it is prudent one understands broad rules that form the tenets of the Islamic system in general. Therefore, in the section below, I have outlined related principles as defined in the Islamic system to be able to then further understand the HR operations and managerial implications.

These sets of principles that Islam prescribes are extendable for setting grounds, procedures, and policies in all HR domains, such as recruitment, training and development, retention, promotions and overall code of conduct policy, and any other HR functions.

Broad Rules Governing Human Resource Practices

The foremost standard in Islamic teachings emphasizes "knowledge and piety." Islam recognizes only piety and knowledge as the touchstones of superiority. Certainly the inference is that any other parameter is not worthy of note or consideration. Before I fully deliberate on this subject, I will let you read narrations from various Islamic sources to illustrate the importance of good conduct and the measures of dominance. Just to quickly refresh readers on how this is linked to HR discussion; the issue of standards in conduct is directly linked to one's performance and dominance to work hierarchy, gender, caste, color, and creed priority. It is narrated in the Holy Quran:

> *O mankind! Truly we have created you male and female and have made you nations and tribes that you may know one another. Indeed the noblest of you in the sight of God is the best in conduct.* (49: 13)

In his last sermon the prophet (pbuh) announced:

> An Arab has no superiority over a non-Arab nor a non-Arab any superiority over an Arab; also a white has no superiority over black nor a black has any superiority over white except by piety and good action.

> A citizen of Balkh[14] says: "I was present before Imam Ali Riza. The time for dinner came. The dining-cloth was spread and meals were served.

The Holy Imam invited all his white and black-skinned servants and without any hesitation seated himself amongst them. Some people suggested a separate dining-cloth for the servants. At this the Holy Imam said: 'We all have One Lord. We all belong to common parents. On the Day of Judgment we all shall be treated equally for our virtues and sins. Then why should there be discrimination here?'"[15]

Islam's Call on Gender Preference

In the Islamic perspective, gender cannot also be a reason of superiority, and no evaluation in any field of accomplishment can be tied to a specific gender. However, what must be explained here very clearly is that although Islam treats a man and a woman equally in their achievements, it does entirely respect the difference in their needs due to physical dissimilarity and physiological needs. Thus, in the Islamic work domain, a man is expected to perform heavy-duty tasks and a woman is relieved of such occupations. The explicit statement on the issue of gender equality is found in the Holy Quran as follows:

> *In the Islamic perspective, gender cannot also be a reason of superiority, and no evaluation in any field of accomplishment can be tied to a specific gender.*

> *Whoever, be it a male or a female, does good deeds and he or she is a believer, then they will enter the Paradise.* (Quran 4: 124)

The guiding principles of equality in terms of gender, caste, color, and creed help set lofty standards, which define the standards for all tasks encompassed within the HR sphere. This loudly and clearly announces a non-discrimination policy and denies any indication or attempt of superiority claims. The emphasis is on no prejudice, thereby helping restore balance in society as this is acknowledged as a principle. How does then one climb ranks and ladders? The status raising standard is also clearly spelt out. It is one's own conduct. Within the organizational setting, one's own conduct is one's performance and

> *The underlying theology of Islamic principles of knowledge and piety, and non-discrimination is extendable and offers concrete guidelines for HR functions.*

the verse and quotation above specify that good action raises one's position and prominence. In the organizational setting, "good" is defined clearly in the form of job descriptions and assigned responsibilities.

This discussion contains the entire work philosophy that an organization that wishes to turn to Islamic perspectives in HR can practice: observing a non-discrimination policy and expecting employees to perform to the best of their abilities.

As we build up the HR practices from the Islamic perspective, Step 2 guides us as follows:

Step 2

- Organization: No prejudice in any category
- Employee: Offers the best conduct to expect any raise in status

Hence two stages can be visualized that can form the basis for developing HR functions within an organization. The accountability principle drives workers to perform to their utmost and finest abilities, given that the organization has set a clear remuneration/reward structure. Once the worker is up and working to the required standards, the organization must ensure that there is no prejudice in whatsoever form (gender, race, class, color, creed) and at all times offer rewards on the basis of the best conduct (performance).

Learning Check: Be Sure You Can

- Explain the principle of non-discrimination and its managerial implications.
- Explain the principle of equality and its managerial implications.

Study Question

What insights come from the accountability concept, present in the Islamic HR perspective?

Management Hierarchy in Islam

The HR department works within the structure in any organization. Within the structure, employees are ranked at various levels. Hierarchy is an important constituent within the structure of any organization. The levels of hierarchy refer to the managerial levels in the organization. Islam too encourages management hierarchy. The balance between workers of different capabilities is referred to as the necessary spirit of natural cooperation and balance in society. In Chapter 43 in the Holy Quran, it is noted:

We have apportioned among them their livelihood in the life of the world, and raised some of them above others in rank that some of them take labour from others. (Quran 43: 32)

This verse refers to the reality of the social situation in which each individual has a different capacity and different talents: those who are superior in one domain tend to engage the cooperation of or employ others for their ultimate mutual benefit. The clear understanding that can be taken forward for managerial implication from this verse is the levels in an organization. These may arise due to differing knowledge strata, experiences, educational qualifications, and such related factors. This concept has multifold dimensions and implications; within the western/contemporary management, this is a key concept via which organization structuring takes place. The vertical hierarchy is based on the degree of specialization, which is exactly what is reflected in the Quranic (from the Holy Quran) verse, that is, the allocated share of one's occupation is defined in levels either raised or otherwise. These specialist competencies also form the basis of different kinds of professional treatment for employees, such as job description, that is, spread of duties and responsibilities, performance management systems such as appraisals resulting in training and development, promotions, or both.

The other premise from the verse above is the implication on the rights of people in

> Islam reflects on the practical social situation in which each individual has a different capacity and different talents: those who are superior in one domain tend to engage the cooperation or employ others for their ultimate mutual benefit.

general and employee relations in particular that develops as a result of the ranking in any environment. The discussion is not completely out of scope of the text; however, because employee relations are not covered in detail, a brief note is added for readers to follow: the stance of a worker in an Islamic environment (whether public or private) is expected to maintain the predefined standards prescribed in the holy sources and this needs to be similar. The settings do not matter. This is because salvation is attained only when one fulfills the rights of God and the rights of other human beings as well.

The clear managerial implication is how to best develop worker interaction that arises within an organization setting as a result of structuring. The functions under worker interaction relate to coordination, delegation, and control mechanisms at the workplace. These as specified above are not going to be the main discussion in the text.

Progression in Work Settings

Following on from hierarchy in an organization, the natural course of progression should be how workers can advance up the vertical ladder, that is, move up the hierarchy. Therefore, what we are going to study from here on is the progress of a worker within an organization.

To be able to comprehend the usual practices and expectation vis-à-vis employee development, let us go through a typical scenario:

> Let me introduce to you Chris (employee) and Ahmad (boss). Chris is a fresh graduate and Ahmad is his supervisor in the graduate trainee program. Through the scenario below, you shall be able to observe the process under study.

Chris has been guided into the organizational setting and is now offered a permanent position to work under Ahmad. Ahmad has been a good supervisor, offering comprehensible advice during the graduate trainee program; hence Chris is happy with the opportunity as he wants to grow into a leader. Aware of Chris's future plans, Ahmad has made sure that Chris is seated near his office and has assured full support as this would be a feather in his cap as a supervisor, should Chris achieve his aims. To be able to achieve any junior leadership position, Ahmad has assigned Chris a project report task, where he is expected to collect data from the entire department and collate it in the form of a report on his own. This, according to Ahmad, is a perfect opportunity and platform for Chris to showcase his abilities.

I met Chris recently and he was full of complaints against his supervisor. Things like, "He isn't providing the promised guidance," "How can I be left on my own completely?" "Why is there no feedback from his side?" and the most sensible one (from Chris's perspective) was "If he doesn't see me often enough, how will he know what I am doing and then how will I ever get promoted and rise to the leadership position ever?"

Although seemingly, Chris is not happy with Ahmad's style, it actually makes sense. Ahmad's approach is to offer Chris open space to understand his role fully by himself. And as expected, when Chris takes on a leadership role in future, he would be required to create a vision for the team he is in charge of, which he can practice now by taking charge of himself and his own vision (of moving to a leadership role). Ahmad is also assuming that Chris has understood the approach (i.e., the freedom provided to him) and would accordingly take advantage of it. Meanwhile, Chris is surely not happy, since he was looking for step-by-step guidance to progress in his career.

As Chris's review is just around the corner, he has a feeling that the outcome is not going to be very positive. Ahmad's stance was to put Chris in charge of his career development, whereas Chris assumed that this responsibility was that of the supervisor.

Whose Responsibility Is It Anyway?

Subordinates generally resort to the blame game. Professionals more than often assume that the level in hierarchy above is responsible for their development. From the western/contemporary management view, organizations are becoming more active in creating career development programs as part of HR development program efforts. Many organizations are designing career programs in an attempt to increase overall organizational performance and employee productivity, and attract, develop, and retain the most qualified employees. The organizational initiative in developing career development programs for workers actually means the organization is responsible for workers' progress. Further, as mentioned above, organizations shall put in place only those programs that match its overall objectives. However, from the Islamic perspective, personal efforts have a great deal of importance. To begin understanding the Islamic perspective of growth and development of an employee, I quote the following verse from the Holy Quran which is found in Chapter 13:

> *Allah does not change the condition of people until they change their own condition.* (Quran 13: 11)

The verse above creates a cause and effect relationship. It clearly explicates that without one's own effort in a given scenario, Allah (SWT) does not simply change man's condition via a miracle. And not only does the verse denies miraculous change in condition; in addition, it straightforwardly identifies that the starting point for any change should be one's own will to change, that is, "realization of the need to change." And further, the verse clearly indicates that initiation of change in condition must come from one's own desire and will. When I went through this verse, I could envisage that in any such situation where human beings are advised to take on the onus of change, there must be guidelines that can help steer one to self-progress? Interestingly, I came across a saying of the holy prophet (pbuh) that provided the key: the starting point of self-progress. And the saying goes as follows:

> Self-appraisal is linked to recognizing God and is considered to be the starting point for anyone who wishes to progress.

> The starting point of self-progress is self-appraisal and exercising self-appraisal implies total evaluation.

According to this quotation, the model can now be refined as follows: At the starting point, any self-progress shall begin with the realization of change and followed by a decision of self-progress. Anyone who determines the need of progression must then draw on self-appraisal, which is equal to recognizing God. Hence we have the model in Figure 4.1.

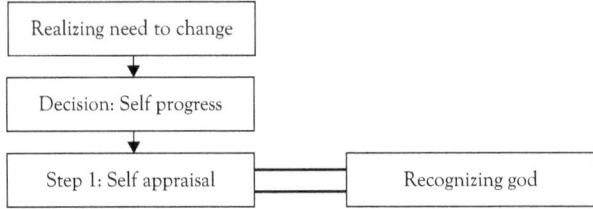

Figure 4.1 Starting self-progress

Progress of a Worker

Putting the pieces together and exercising self-appraisal implies total evaluation. And because the overall aim is to be close (*qurbat*) to Allah (SWT) (should be understood as spiritual closeness), an appraisal shall help the appraisee recognize God. When a person tries to acquire Allah's (SWT) closeness, it eventually leads him or her to start acquainting with the religious tenets. And as discussed above, one of the religious tenets is that failure to perfect your work when you are sure of the reward is injustice to yourself. Therefore as quoted from Imam Ali, "One who realizes one's own self realizes his Lord." In the wider perspective, this is a means to develop, enhance, and progress one's own self.

Recall from discussions in the previous chapters, the Islamic stance does not consider human conduct to differ in the sphere of their public and private lives. Hence the work front is not treated as a separate element of one's life. Hence, although the title of this section is "Progress of a Worker" it is just so as to help the readers connect to employees and their progress. In essence, the visual in Figure 4.1 applies to anyone who realizes the need to initiate a self-change process. The same can be translated into a department change insinuated by the head of the department who assumes the responsibility "realizing need to change" in his role and capacity.

Narrowing it down to the HR perspective, if following a self-appraisal one realizes the need to move forward and progress can only be achieved through gaining new skills and upgrading knowledge, in actuality, it is a movement toward perfection and hence is completely in line with the teachings of the Holy Quran. Have a look at the verse below:

> *Are those who have knowledge equal to those who do not have knowledge?!* (Quran 39: 9)

The Holy Quran provides a wake-up call to human beings by questioning how the two extremes can be the same. Certainly not, and the liked one is the one who possesses knowledge.

Developing the diagram further (Figure 4.2), that explains how realizing the need to change is linked to knowledge acquisition (KA). The western equivalent terminology for knowledge acquisition is training needs.

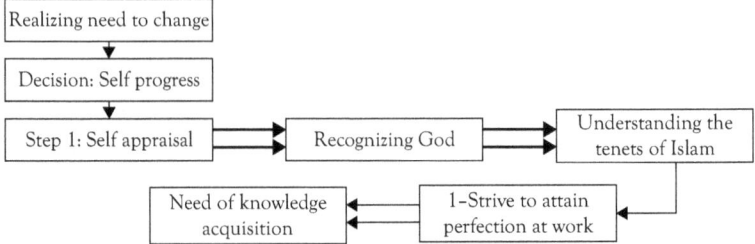

Figure 4.2 The need to change is linked to the need of knowledge acquisition

Linking the ideas from Figures 4.1 and 4.2, from the Islamic perspective, self-appraisal is gauged and set to be equivalent to the recognition of Allah (SWT), which in essence means understanding the teachings and principles of Islam. One of these as discussed above is to strive and attain perfection at work, to achieve which, one may seek to opt for KA.

Learning Check: Be Sure You Can

- Describe how both the Islamic and the western school of management share the concept of management hierarchy.
- Apply the concept to see how managers can work up the hierarchy ladder.
- Explain how self-progress is linked to self-appraisal.
- Explain when self-appraisal is connected to knowledge acquisition.

Study Questions

1. From the Islamic perspective, whose responsibility is career progress and how does this link to knowledge acquisition (training and development)?
2. How does the Islamic perspective link management hierarchy and balance in the society?

Knowledge Acquisition

The significant element in the illustration above is the final step of "knowledge acquisition," which is the term used in the Islamic scriptures and teachings with reference to any sort of upgrade in learning. The Islamic term associated with theory of knowledge is "ilm" and it encompasses a much larger meaning. When looking at a synonym for "ilm" in order to translate it into English, training does not seem to suffice. We shall therefore make use of the term "knowledge" in order to understand "ilm."

To begin deliberating on this vast subject (I do not intend to uncover the various kinds of "ilm" and its facets in this text; this is because it is surely out of scope of this text. I just provide a hint, and those interested can search for different kinds of ilm), it is prudent to understand the importance of "ilm" in Islamic tenets. The holy prophet has announced gaining "ilm" knowledge as obligatory to all Muslims, both men and female. There are numerous places in the Holy Quran where the emphasis on gaining knowledge is stressed. In addition, there are scores of prophetic traditions that encourage Muslims to acquire all types of knowledge from any corner of the world, even if that means going to China (China symbolizes any far-flung place, reaching which is filled with hardships as in the times of the holy prophet); so much so that the holy prophet (pbuh) has specified what is knowledge as outlined below.

> The Islamic term associated with theory of knowledge is "*ilm*" and it encompasses a much larger meaning.

Knowledge as Defined by the Holy Prophet (pbuh)

When the holy prophet of God was asked: "What is knowledge?" he replied: "To keep silent." He was asked: "Then?" He said: "To listen attentively." He was asked: "Then?" He said: "To remember." He was asked: "Then?" He said: "To act upon (what is learned)." He was asked: "Then?" He said: "To propagate."[16]

The model depicting the process of knowledge acquisition (see Figure 4.3) needs to be further reflected upon.

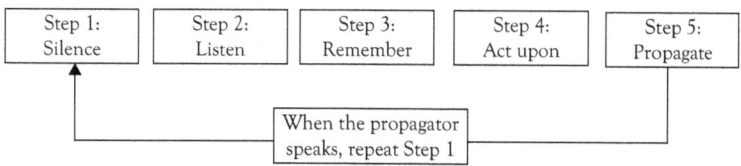

Figure 4.3 *The knowledge acquisition process*

Take this as a class exercise if you are teaching this course in a college or if you are a trainer of Islamic perspectives on HR. Use this as the first brainstorming exercise in your group of attendees and begin by asking them—How do they think one acquires knowledge?

Collect all answers on a whiteboard and identify keywords. Now introduce the model to the participants and commence discussion, aligning the explanation with any keywords that match with the model.

The model is uncomplicated. It is a common fact that to be able to concentrate, one needs to be quiet, so that the brain doesn't have to multitask. And this is then followed by listening (in itself, active listening is a vast subject). Acting upon what has been understood is deemed extremely important in Islamic teachings before propagating because, according to Islam, there is no weightage and consequence for a mere saying that is not practiced. One must practice what is being preached.

Prophet and Dates Story

Once a woman brought his son to the holy prophet (pbuh) asking him to instruct his son not to eat lots of dates. The holy prophet (pbuh) asked her to return after 3 days. The woman brought her son after 3 days and then the prophet helped her as she had asked. Upon her inquiring why the prophet did not instruct her son the same day, he explained that the particular day she brought him he himself was eating dates and how could he have asked a young boy not to do something he was practicing in front of the boy. Clearly, the message is to act upon before propagating.

Learning Check: Be Sure You Can

- Discuss the different arrays of schools within the western concepts of HRM.
- Describe the importance of HRM from an Islamic perspective.

Study Question

What is the importance of silence, listening, and acting upon in the Islamic process of knowledge acquisition model?

Knowledge Acquisition Department

Knowledge acquisition is the closest equivalent term to the contemporary training and development terminology within the HR domain. From the Islamic viewpoint, the element of knowledge acquisition (training and development) is a devotee's act and is highly encouraged; this can be tracked from the following saying of the holy prophet (pbuh):

> Acquire knowledge, because he who acquires it, in the way of the Lord, performs an act of piety; who speaks of it praises the Lord; who seeks it, adores God, who dispenses instruction in it, bestows alms; and who imparts it to its fitting objects, performs an act of devotion to God. Knowledge enables its possessor to distinguish what is forbidden from what is not.

The saying above can be analyzed to understand the significance of KA from the perspective of involved entities.

Knowledge Attainment Should Be in the Way of God

There is an unambiguous message conveyed. Knowledge advancement by an individual cannot be solely for worldly progress; as a matter of fact, the intention is "closeness to God." This connects quite well, using the quotations above; one without knowledge cannot be equated to the one who does not. And if knowledge is sought in the way of God it is equal to an act of piety. Recalling from the prophet's last sermon, no one has superiority but based on their degree of piety. Creating the HR implication is simple; yes, from the Islamic perspective knowledge achievement has a lofty status, which also assists in climbing the hierarchy ladder in any organization.

Who Speaks of It Praises the Lord

Whosoever propagates the merits of or develops people's interest in any training program is as if he is honoring God. This act of selling the training program and convincing others to be trained and acquire knowledge is equated with praising the Lord. This particular segment of the saying opens up a position in any KA department, that of someone who explains to the prospective trainees the value of KA. From the western school of thought perspective, if an organization offers a training program and if employees are convinced about the associated worth, then this should result in a cohort of people interested in being trained.

Who Dispenses the Instruction, Bestows Alms

The role of a trainer who is serving people to improvise their knowledge base is as if he is donating and offering charity in the path of God. Giving charity is a highly likeable act in Islam and the general impression is that this is only possible via distributing wealth. The mystification is clarified and the lofty status of a trainer is elucidated through this saying.

Who Imparts It to Its Fitting Objects, Performs an Act of Devotion to God

The process does not halt and the larger good of the society is charted out. The clear implication of the likeable act for a trained employee is to further impart the acquired knowledge to other colleagues, family, or community, and if he or she does that, then it is as if he or she has performed a devotee act to God.

All in all, KA is a dispersion process (see Figure 4.4), where at each step the involved employee is seen to be performing a religious act. In this manner, the Quran and prophet's Sunnah address their teachings to mankind at large and affirm that every man may improve himself through knowledge.

> Knowledge acquisition is a dispersion process, where at each step the involved employee is seen to be performing a religious act.

The knowledge attainment department (training and development department)—Islamic perspective.

How Does Islamic Knowledge Acquisition Compare With Training and Development in Western Schools of Thought?

In contemporary management, HRM represents a new and radically different way of managing people and is a critical lever for improving

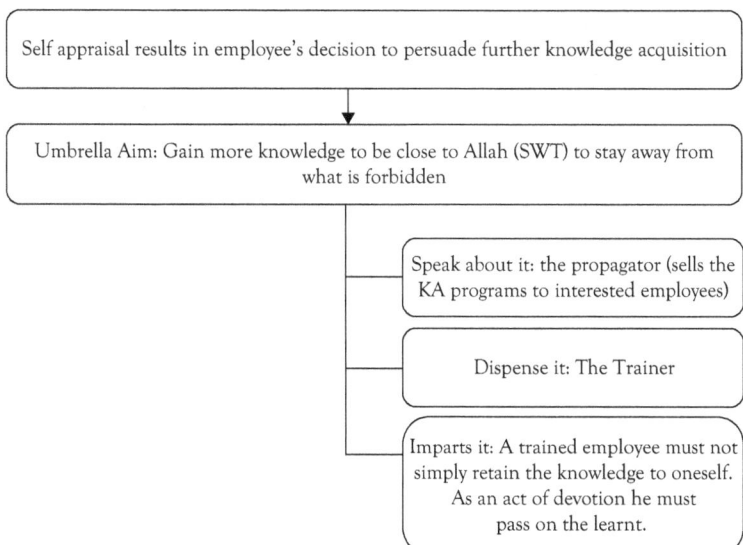

Figure 4.4 The knowledge acquisition process and entities

organizational performance (Storey, 2007). The onus of training and development resides with the organization that decides what kind of edification is suitable based on market needs and the overall aims of the organization. Where this is beneficial to the employee, the larger beneficiary is the organization. By the same token, if the organization works on number crunching, any other economic reasons, or both, training may just be eliminated. The HR department in the western school of thought may sometimes just act upon economic reasons and overlook the human aspect entirely. The Islamic perspective of KA on the other hand provides for a much larger gain and is more purposeful. Further, inspired by the fact that the purpose of knowledge gain is being close to God, its recipient advances the obtained knowledge and this results in the spread of it to the general community.

Broad Differences Between Islamic and Western Perspectives on HRM

From the discussion above, it can be easily gathered that the Islamic perspectives are all-encompassing and tend to look at the umbrella objective of gaining closeness to Allah (SWT). A short summary of concepts studied

Table 4.1 Human resource management—differences in perspectives

Western/contemporary human resources perspective	Quotations used from the Islamic literature	Islamic human resources perspective
Human resources are externally controlled by line managers and other sources as identified in the structure of any given organization.	"Everyone is entangled in the outcome of his deeds." (Surah al-Muddath-thir 74: 38)	All human beings are accountable to Allah (SWT) for their actions (an act is any occurrence in one's private or public life).
Organization is responsible to keep creating motivating factors to help employees feel secure at the workplace.	Imam Ali, in Nahjul-Balagha (p. 483) stated, "Persist in your action with a noble end in mind…. Failure to perfect your work while you are sure of the reward is injustice to yourself."	The fact that a worker in the Islamic business environment is accountable to Allah (SWT) makes him or her intrinsically motivated to perform based on the agreed rewards.
Organization is responsible for workers' career progress.	Self-appraisal is linked to recognizing God and is considered to be the starting point for anyone who wishes to progress (holy prophet's saying).	The onus of progressing in life in general and career in particular lies with the worker.

in this chapter is provided (see Table 4.1) as a comparison between the western/contemporary school of thought and the Islamic viewpoint. In order to create a reminder for readers, the quotations used in the text above are provided in the second column.

The information in the table clearly ascertains the differences between the Islamic and the western/contemporary schools of thought. Nevertheless, there are similarities between the two philosophies as well, where the working methodology to achieve the desired parameter may be different and can be termed operational differences.

Summary

The value of HRM as a function in the Islamic school of thought can be understood from the fact that Islamic prescription views the interests of employees and employers as complementary. This is fairly similar to the resource-based view of HR within the western/contemporary

HR perspective. The concept of accountability in the Islamic belief system emphasizes that one is responsible for one's own actions and hence both employers and employees are answerable. The very notion of accountability is translated and viewed across the range of conduct. The broad rules governing HR practices are knowledge and piety, equality in gender, caste, color, and creed. Any hierarchy in an organization, defined as an organization structure that is dependent on qualifications, job descriptions, and work allocation of employees is in agreement with the IM system; however, the criteria of ranks must be defined under the factors in agreement with Islamic premise.

From the Islamic perspective, a worker must take initiative for one's career growth and development via self-appraisal. If the self-appraisal exercise results in self-progress, then it must culminate in a desire to acquire knowledge, where real knowledge according to the holy prophet (pbuh) is one that is put into action. All KA departments must keep the umbrella aim of offering their training programs in the way of God and not just worldly gains.

CHAPTER 5

The Islamic Perspective on Leadership

Leadership is a much researched topic in the western/contemporary school. From charismatic, transactional, transformational, and servant leadership theories, which were the most extensively discussed, the focus has now moved to the ethical and moral dimension of leadership.[1-3] Hunt and Conger assert that the range of new leadership conceptions is quite abroad. In the western/contemporary school of thought, leadership is big on the agenda.[4] In addition to leadership principles emerging and hailed by top corporations, many leadership gurus are publishing both in leading journals and authoring full texts on the subject.

There are a wide variety of theoretical constructs around the concept, which generally begin by a discussion on trait leadership, which is defined as a set of properties individuals portray as inborn characteristics; some also include physical factors and other characteristics as part of the discussion on trait theory of leadership. Nevertheless, there is another view on leadership that identifies it as a process that involves interaction between leaders and followers. This perspective makes leadership a learned behavior.

The scope of leadership has been researched from many perspectives such as culture, situation, spirituality, and religious leadership. It is not uncommon to find studies on leadership based on ethical, Christianity, Judaism, and Islamic perspectives. In an interesting article in a leading journal on leadership, the central thesis was that in each of the major religious traditions of the world, there are indications of a common underlying multiple level ontology of spiritual leadership, which can be, and is applied in organizational settings.[5]

From the Islamic perspective, the leadership theme is given substantial significance. We shall draw evidence of leadership from the Holy Quran and the life of the holy prophet (pbuh), and the Islamic literature available as explained in an earlier part of the text. In the life of the holy prophet (pbuh), Muslims have a thorough role model. The Quran also verifies this statement and states that he is the best of leaders according to the following verse:

> *For you the life of the Prophet is a good model of behavior.* (Quran 33: 21)

Indeed, for the purpose of understanding Islamic leadership, I will therefore in addition to the verses of the Holy Quran, be utilizing actions from the life of Prophet Muhammad (pbuh) and his companions who offer excellent leadership models. Specifically, I shall utilize the compilation titled "Peak of Eloquence"—an English translation of the book titled *Nahjul-Balagha* containing the sermons, letters, and traditions as quoted by Holy Ali (A.S.[6]) who was a close comrade of the holy prophet (S.A.W.) and the fourth righteous caliph. Moghaddam and Gholamzadeh[7] express the significance of the text by saying, "*Nahjul-Balagha* is similar to a precious counsel in the humanities' hands that depicts the visage of a perfect human and a meritorious society in all of its chapters which depict the sketch of four seasons as a beautiful painting."

The approach taken should therefore help readers understand how leaders should be from the Islamic perspective and thus what leadership entails. To begin with, I shall be looking into Islamic leadership principles. Early research defines Islamic leadership principles as a group of leadership principles that were extracted primarily from the Quran and the biography of the Prophet Muhammad and his companions for the orientation of governmental affairs and the construction of good and ethical leadership to guide Islamic leaders in running Islamic organizations appropriately and effectively. The point to be remembered is that, what distinguishes Islamic leadership most from traditional Western notions of leadership is the close attachment of leadership to religion, especially its moral and human roots.[8]

The importance of leadership can be judged from the following saying: the holy prophet (pbuh) has said that if two (or three) persons travel together, they should choose one of them as their chief and manager. This tradition shows the extent of importance Islam attaches to leadership and to discipline. In another tradition, it is narrated on the authority of Abu Dawud[9] that, the holy prophet emphasized the importance of having a leader; Muslims must appoint a leader during a trip, select a leader (*imam*) to lead the prayer, and choose a leader for other group activities.

There is clarity on the understanding that leadership is a much larger responsibility and mere management is perfectly adequate when routine operations are in action. The concept of leadership is therefore developed in many varied ways to observe how effective leadership is successful in bringing about change.

From the Islamic Lens What Is Leadership All About?

I begin with a quotation by Imam Ali from the text in *NahjulBalagha* as follows:

> Whoever wants to be a leader should educate himself before educating others. Before preaching to others he should first practice himself. Whoever educates himself and improves his own morals is superior to the man who tries to teach and train others.[10]

There are quite a few interesting facts that can be gathered from the quotation above in the context of organizational leadership and leadership implication:

1. One can desire to be a leader, that is, leadership is an art that can be learned like any other arts.
2. Once leadership is desired, the first step is to educate oneself, followed by educating the followers.
3. What is learned by the leadership must be practiced (for what is not practiced, refer to the model in KA department).
4. And a final statement on the dominance of the educated one: one who works on developing himself morally is surely superior versus one who resorts to just teaching others without practicing the learning himself.

I shall take forward the understanding from the quotation above that leadership is an art that can be learned. In the western/contemporary management, it is well known that the leadership paradigm is changing, and a leadership model based on ethical principles is finally emerging.

Interestingly this is the position that Islam has taken from the start. The belief in ethical values as prescribed by Islam takes precedence in the entire value system. Hence, drawing the basis of leadership from the Islamic perspective, we shall dwell on the life of the prophet to seek guidance and be able to develop a model. I am still utilizing the quotation above, where one of the principles learned is that one who desires to be a leader must practice. Let us look at the example of the holy prophet (pbuh) who pronounced prophethood at the age of 40.

Even before the holy prophet (pbuh) announced his prophethood, his honesty and reliability were very well known. People used to call him Muhammad, the trustworthy. People entrusted their valuables to him for safe custody. Hence the understanding that a sound character is an important element for any future leader who wishes to have his message delivered and followed. Look at the future value; even after the holy prophet (pbuh) announced prophethood in Mecca, despite the fact that not all inhabitants of Mecca picked up Islam they still continued to deposit their valuables with him, for safekeeping. A study conducted by Allison et al. reported that a leader's immoral actions are likely to posthumously stain both the leader's reputation and the organization's image.[11] The organizational implications of a moral leadership are vast and many researchers comment on ethics being at the heart of leadership studies.[12–14] The Islamic principles dictate that even those aspiring to be leaders, in the role of leadership, or both must adhere to honesty and safekeeping.

Leadership learning from the life of the holy prophet (pbuh) as expressed in the Holy Quran and his conduct can be a source of understanding leadership skills for those seeking leadership positions. Thus within the premise of this text we shall be looking at generating Islamic leadership principles that can fairly be referred to as inspirational leadership principles from Islam. What is also important to understand here is that we shall not be dealing the topic in line with the western/contemporary school of management where leadership is of different types; instead the discussion shall identify attributes that predispose an individual to succeed in a leadership role. These are the practiced principles and, as explained above, are the basis of leadership in an Islamic environment. However, in order for the text to be comprehensible for all readers alike, I shall draw from the quotations, sayings, verses and Islamic scriptures, and the life and conduct of the holy prophet, the nature, qualities, behavior, and styles of leaders and leadership as they ought to be. Nevertheless, what must be kept in mind whilst reading the text is that, Islamic leadership is a comprehensive approach and leaders ought to possess the attributes discussed below; weightage of the attributes then leads to developing leadership styles appropriate to organizational perspective. Hence, what needs to be understood in the context of Islamic leadership is that, in Islam, leadership is all about a discernable and marked set of skills and behavior evident via one's actions.

Learning Check: Be Sure You Can

- Discuss the different arrays of concepts associated with leadership within western concepts.
- Describe the importance of leadership from an Islamic perspective.
- Understand the importance of education to leadership in Islam.

Study Questions

1. How can you link the holy prophet's attributes of honesty and reliability to his to be announced prophethood (leadership)?
2. What are the sources of Islamic leadership principles?

Leadership Principles From the Life of the Holy Prophet (pbuh)

I begin to explore for you the leadership principles from the life of the holy prophet (pbuh) using a verse from the third chapter in the holy book, where Allah (SWT) pronounces:

> *It is by the mercy of Allah that you (the Prophet) were lenient to them, for if you had been harsh and hard-hearted, they surely would have left your company. Therefore pardon them and implore Allah to forgive them. And hold consultations with them in regard to the conduct of affairs. Once you are resolved, put your trust in Allah. Allah likes those who put their trust in Him.* (Quran 3: 159)

Analyzing the verse above, holy prophet (pbuh) is realized to be

- an approachable and forgiving leader;
- a thoughtful and tolerant leader who had the utmost concern for his companions as he seeks forgiveness for them.

And analyzing the verse above, there is clarity on the fact that Allah (SWT) desires to see a leader who gives importance to his companions and holds consultations with them.

Example of Prophet's Consultations

The holy prophet (pbuh) used to hold strategic discussions with his companions and he provided them with the opportunity to exercise their intellect in tactical matters such as the first battle of Islam: the battle of Badr. This was an important time for the Muslims since this was the first time the devotees of the new faith were out there in the field defending themselves under the banner of Islam. They were not only few in number as compared to the opponents, they also did not have enough artillery and war animals for transportation. At this critical juncture, the holy prophet (pbuh) consulted with his companions on whether taking military action against the enemy was the right thing to do, where the camping ground should be, and even after the war was over he sought their advice on matters such as how to deal with the prisoners of war.

Because this is not a religious text, narrating the entire incident of the various battles where the prophet sought the advice of his companions, their advice, and the account of the battles is out of scope of the text. But it is worth mentioning that the holy prophet (pbuh) took into consideration the advice of Salman al-Farsi, one of the companions, who hailed from Persia. This was despite the narrow-mindedness and the superiority complex held by Arabs at that time and also given that the prophet himself was an Arab. The lesson from the above discussion is that by embracing diversity in consultations the holy prophet (pbuh) embraced Salman al-Farsi's advice. The holy prophet (pbuh) promoted not only diversity, he preached and practiced parity. His action of acknowledging equality and brotherhood is evident in examples such as one of his closest companions being a former Negro slave, Bilaal; one of his trusted lieutenants was Suhayb from Rome. These followers came from different places, spoke different languages, and were of different heritage. However, in their teacher's company, they were all the same, equal to each other without distinction (Great Prophet, n.d.).

Salman al-Farsi,[15] who knew far more of the techniques of warfare than was common in the Peninsula, advised the digging of a dry moat around Medina and the fortifications of its buildings within. The trench took 6 days to dig and the opponent's army was taken by huge surprise, the trench, an obstacle they did not calculate. It is also worth mentioning that the holy prophet (pbuh) also participated in digging the moat.

From the western/contemporary school of leadership, the practice of seeking advice falls into the category of consultative leadership. Being a consultative leader is all about building confidence in your team, subordinates, or both. And following from the above discussion based on the Holy Quran, the holy prophet's (pbuh) personality is justified of being approachable. The prophet consulted his companions and valued their views, and this was done with the view of helping them develop their personality. However, what does not have an exact parallel in the western/contemporary school is the exercise of leaders engaging in work with the followers; it is more like leading from the front and the closest term to the act is exemplary leadership.

A case of his exemplary leadership was his dynamic and proactive interest in the propagation of Islam. He used to take personal initiative, in addition to sending deputies to Ethiopia and Yemen. Once he went to Taif (a place in Mecca) for this purpose. During the annual pilgrimage season, he used to invite nearby tribes to convey his message of Islam. He sent a good number of his companions to Ethiopia. He also took various initiatives by writing letters to various heads of states to explain his message.

According to the western/contemporary school of leadership, such actions of the holy prophet (pbuh) can be seen as those of a strategic and visionary leader; one who provides vision and direction and makes wise and deliberate choices about how to lead and at the same time, as visionary leaders are, predominantly future-oriented, preemptive, and risk-taking. By definition, these leaders center their decisions and activities on their beliefs and values, and share their value system with the followers. In the case of the holy prophet (pbuh), the long-term vision was spreading the knowhow of Islam in the world. In a span of 23 years, he made this huge task achievable and manageable by sharing the understanding of his vision with his followers. Visionary leaders on the other hand, according to the literature, are focused mainly on the future and the direction their vision should take in future. A combination of visionary and strategic leadership skills can yield progressive results in the short and long run. This is a perfect combination for a leader to possess, strategic and visionary leadership skills. Being a strategic leader implies one is focused toward envisioning a future considering the present set of affairs and in parallel paying attention to short-term stability. A combination of visionary leadership skills implies a leader with an understanding of what is to be achieved in the long term.

From the organizational perspective, the learning is fairly straight onward. For organizations to be effective, a strategic leader must be able to build an expressive long-term vision and work toward achieving it and attempt to communicate their understanding of this desired vision with others in the organization. And a visionary leader is concerned with ensuring the organization's future prospects. This means that a combination of visionary and strategic leadership skills covers the entire continuum of managerial leadership capability. The strategic sect would ensure day-to-day operations run in harmony and the visionary aspect would mean that the focus on the long term is not lost at any point in time.

Another saying of the holy prophet (pbuh) as quoted from Sirah Ibn Hisham—the holy prophet told Mu'az bin Jabal:

> Make things easy for the people; do not make them difficult; win their hearts by telling them pleasing things; do not scare them away; and when you offer prayers with them, your prayers should be such as suit the weakest of them.

The Islamic perspective on leadership skills that can be gathered from the saying above is that the ability of the leader is to be able to simplify both facts and tasks for followers and companions. Expressions that contain jargon may sound impressive but in reality these frighten people away.

The way prescribed to gain people's approval and cause them to understand your vision is to tell them simple things expressed in unpretentious language.

What is the most important learning that can be taken away from the above saying? It refers to leaders whilst they are leading prayers. This is quite symbolic. Muslims offer prayers five times a day and offering prayers in congregation is highly recommended. The holy prophet is clarifying how an Imam (the one who leads prayers) should offer prayers; it should be such that the weakest of those offering prayers behind him should not be at a disadvantage. The prayer leader must consider that the followers (mamoom—those who follow an Imam) do not get tired by too long offerings or that if the prayers are offered to fast, many who are weak or old may not be able to keep pace. The organizational implication can be stretched to many scenarios, ranging from time adherence in meetings to clarity in communication skills, considering the needs of all types of staff that the organization employs. If the organization has a policy of employing workers with special needs or employees nearing retirement age, such a set of workers may have different needs. A leader (who may be the strategic leader) must ensure that no one feels lacking in anything and any communication is correctly understood. Refer back to the "Human Resource Management in Islam" chapter where we have discussed "the knowledge acquisition department" and self-appraisal. A product of self-appraisal by a leader may well be a need to communicate such that all followers are treated with parity. This identified training need then goes through the process of actual KA. Recall the last step in the KA process (human resource management in Islam) where the one who acquires knowledge then has the duty to further impart it; hence the leader must propagate the learned skills.

Learning Check: Be Sure You Can

- Describe consultative leadership from the Islamic perspective.
- Understand how the Islamic leadership can be both visionary and strategic.
- Explain simplicity in communication skills of a leader as a desired attribute.

Study Questions

1. How does the combination of strategic and visionary leadership yield progressive results?
2. How can a leader ensure that the weakest subordinate is not disadvantaged?

Education and Leaders—The Islamic Perspective

From the Islamic perspective on leadership, the third and the most stressed point is "Education." Prophet Muhammad emphasized the prominence of education, decreeing education as a must for all people, irrespective of any gender restrictions (male or female). How does education assist the leader and the followers?

From the Islamic lens, the merit of the "Alim" (the learned) over the "Abid" (the devout) is like the merit of the moon over the stars on a full-moon night.[16]

Therefore, if the leader remains "the learned" and continuously strives to learn, propagates the learning amongst the followers, the workforce is more apropos to take on the modern day challenges. Stress on education means further focus on developing the followers and helping them grow through edification; it also means leaders in Islam are required to show concern for companions and followers, that is, they are by nature required to be "compassionate leaders." As a compassionate leader, the holy prophet (pbuh) understood the needs of the time and knowing that encouraging knowledge will help his followers gain an edge, he stimulated his companions to focus on attaining knowledge and gaining literary skills and, as mentioned above as a religious command, he pronounced that it was incumbent on children to learn reading and writing.

One of his sayings, again emphasizing that knowledge has no boundaries—he specifically said:

Wherever you find a useful piece of knowledge, acquire it. It does not matter if you find it with a disbeliever or a hypocrite.

What needs to be understood at this point is that compassionate leaders do not just mean kind leaders. It is about living up to the responsibility placed on their shoulders. His own method of disseminating his message and preaching was gentle and warm, not tough and severe. He filled his companion with hope and refrained from simply scaring them away. To the deputies who he would send to far-flung areas to preach and convey his message, he would specifically provide instructions such as:

> *Be pleasant and do not be harsh. Tell the people what may please them and do not make them disgusted.*

The holy prophet (pbuh) addressed all issues striking the right balance, applying his power positively with passion. Surely it was his farsightedness, compassion, and visionary leadership that helped Muslims develop their strength and base speedily.

Loyal and Passionate Employees or Loyal and Passionate Leaders

From the organizational perspective, organizations are always on the outlook for loyal and passionate employees. Interestingly, such is possible in employees when the manager/leader himself or herself is also dedicated and passionate! There's a powerful link between productivity and what has been identified as "compassionate leadership" in organizations according to a research study conducted by a lecturer at the Australian School of Business.[17] The study looked at the links between leadership and organizational performance. According to the study, the single greatest influence on profitability and productivity within an organization is the ability of leaders to spend more time and effort developing and recognizing their people, welcoming feedback, including criticism, and fostering co-operation among staff (as revealed by data from more than 5,600 people in 77 organizations). This is quite in line with the discussion above and also further deliberation to follow.

Taking on from the success factors identified in the study above, as a leader the holy prophet (pbuh) was patient with his followers. He had the tolerance required to listen to comments even if they were mere criticism. Occasionally he had to face the criticism of his companions, but his way forward was always to explain his side of the story and explain to them as to why a certain decision was taken. Through his communication skills, he would explain his decision without being harsh to them and help them understand the situation at hand; this would then result in their agreement. One of the things however, that he stood steadfast in was his displeasure toward flattery and uncalled-for praises. As a sign of abhorrence, he used to say: "Throw dust on the face of the flatterers."

The Major Principle of Islamic Leadership Is Consistency and Orderliness

The holy prophet's (pbuh) actions were all directed by the utmost regularity. All his activities were worked around a timetable that would have a fine balance between his family life, time devoted to speeches and teachings to his companions, and offering religious preaching. This included a part of every night being devoted to saying prayers, to worship. His daily activities were arranged in such a manner leaving no room for idleness. He did not approve of wasting time and used to say:

> *O' Allah! I take refuge in you from laziness, lethargy, disability and worthlessness.*

In today's competitive world, leaders need to possess the utmost disciplinary skills. Discipline is a thoughtful attribute and in essence it is a large aspect in great leaders. A follower would only want to be disciplined within the rules or guidelines of the organization and not feel resentful if the leader practices the same.

The holy prophet (pbuh) was a principled leader, and withstood all threats, challenges, and difficulties in the hardest of financial predicaments. He showed consistency in completing his task of spreading his message despite the threatening environment. The perfect example is the famous words of the holy prophet (pbuh) which were uttered after the chiefs of Quraysh (tribe in the city of Medina where the prophet was propagating his mission) reached out to the holy prophet's (pbuh) uncle Abu Talib. They openly asked Abu Talib to stop his nephew from spreading his message and threatened him to take the holy prophet's life if he didn't stop his mission. When his uncle conveyed the message, the holy prophet of Islam remarked,

> I swear by Almighty God that even if they put the sun in my right hand and the moon in my left, and in return, demand of me to quit the propagation of Islam and pursuance of my divine aim, I will never do what they want me to. I am determined to carry on my duty toward God to the last moment of my life, even if it means losing my life. I am strongly determined to attain my goal.

The Quraysh then even tried to entice the holy prophet (pbuh) by offering him money, wealth, position, and power, but to their utter disappointment he was found firm in performing his duty.

Perseverance as an Islamic Leadership Principle

From his life then the leadership principle is that of showing perseverance, willpower, and belief in his mission. It is evident that he was able to display a wonderful willpower. The total period of his mission as a prophet contains lessons of perseverance, where his mission took precedence over any other striving in the way. In the endeavor toward fulfilling his mission, a number of times the conditions seemed hopeless but he never let the word failure reach his mind. He stayed steadfast and showed enormous willpower.

From the western/contemporary leadership approach, leadership does have a moral dimension and whenever leaders need to make an ethical decision, it is often the willpower of a leader that helps him or her make the decision with morality. The social psychologist Roy Baumeister argues that willpower is a quality that predicts positive outcomes in many areas of life, and ranks it as one of the most important factors in this respect.[18] Within the study of leadership, lack of willpower may affect a leader's ability to act morally.[19] Hence, perseverance and willpower are studied under moral leadership in the contemporary school of management and leadership studies.

The Islamic Leader Delegates

As a leader, he was able to identify his companions and followers' skills based on which he distributed the tasks. After he migrated to Medina, he formed the Islamic state and systematized a special secretariat, and formed groups of people for performing different tasks. For example, one group of people scribed the revelation, some of the people chosen were assigned the job of drafting letters, yet another group logged legal transactions, and others kept financial records. These examples elucidate that Islamic leadership is all about developing people to their fullest potential.

It is a commonly known fact that a good leader should be able to delegate; it is essential to remember that although a leader distributes work, he is still held accountable. Now, that is the key; delegation does not imply dumping jobs on subordinates. Successful delegation in the organizational perspective means employee empowerment. And at the same time, it helps the leader free up his time for more pressing issues. Because a leader is still accountable, delegation is also about the leader knowing his subordinate's skill set. If the job is assigned to the right person, not only will it get done correctly but it will also make the subordinate confident and add to his or her self-esteem. On the other hand, if leaders believe they are the only ones who can do things right, they do not let their workers develop. The old saying fits here: "Feed a man a fish, feed him for the day, teach a man to fish, feed him for a lifetime."

What must not be forgotten is that involved and engaged workers feel motivated and feel the ownership of the undertaking.

At this point, it would be prudent if readers could connect the HR aspect here, that is—How does a leader delegate tasks? The factors to consider should well fit in with self-appraisal by workers. An exercise that shall assist them to understand their knowledge and skills as they fit the task and what they may wish to progress into, and thus develop their knowledge and skills is the "knowledge acquisition department."

The Charismatic Leadership in Islam

True charisma from the Islamic perspective is in one's conduct. It is quoted from verse 33 of the Holy Quran:

Most certainly, you (people) have in the messenger of Allah an excellent pattern (of behavior). (Quran 33: 21)

And in sermon 103 in "Peak of Eloquence," Imam Ali has been quoted; whilst describing the holy prophet (pbuh) he said:

> Then Allah deputized Muhammad (S.A.) as a witness, giver of good tidings and warner, the best in the universe as a child and the chastest as a grown up man, the purest of the purified in conduct, and the most generous of those who are approached for generosity.

Learning Check: Be Sure You Can

- Describe compassionate leadership from the Islamic perspective
- Relate to a leader's call on discipline.
- Explain the importance of a leader's ability to withstand threats and challenges.
- Explain the role of delegation as an attribute of good leadership.
- Understand charismatic leadership in Islam.

Study Questions

1. What is the moral dimension of leadership from the Islamic perspective?
2. How is delegating a task related to the activities of the knowledge acquisition department?

Leadership Advice From Imam Ali

To take the discussion forward, I shall now utilize Imam Ali's letter advising Malik Ashtar (his governor to be) when he was being sent to lead the people of Egypt. This particular letter is being used to derive leadership implications from an organization perspective by generalizing the rules mentioned. For this purpose, excerpts from the letter have been used below.

Imam Ali advises as follows:

> Develop in your heart the feeling of love for your people and let it be the source of kindliness and blessing to them. Do not behave with them like a barbarian, and do not appropriate to yourself that which belongs to them.

Certainly the recommendation for a leader is to lead the people with something beyond self. The Islamic leadership is not about the leader's greed, ego, or arrogance—it's about showing care for your subordinates. This explanation is quite similar to the concept of compassionate leaders as gathered from the life of the holy prophet (pbuh); the added description is the behavioral aspect of a leader, which should not be ruthless and inhumane. As Imam Ali explains, do not take away from your followers/workers what is theirs. This is the quality of a beast; it seizes and snatches what belongs to others. The Imam has compared this to a barbaric act, meaning the leader should not be uncultured, ignorant, and cruel. The Islamic leader ought to display humanity values. The reason that the Imam explains a leader should display compassion is given below (although the Imam has used "citizens of state," we are generalizing this to the common man, since after all it refers to mankind). Imam Ali said:

> Remember that the citizens of the state are of two categories. They are either your brethren in religion or your brethren in kind. They are subject to infirmities and liable to commit mistakes. Some indeed do commit mistakes. But forgive them even as you would like God to forgive you. Bear in mind that you are placed over them, even as I am placed over you. And then there is God even above him who has given you the position of a Governor in order that you may look after those under you and to be sufficient unto them. And you will be judged by what you do for them.

The reason the Imam has given for leaders to be kind and forgiving is fairly logical; he says that all human beings are similar, either followers of the same faith or of the same kind (which means all humans are the same in needs, requirements, in the way their physical form is defined). Now that is very simple; it's all about treating people as equal human beings. Imam Ali has further stressed the point that humans by their very nature are subject to committing errors, but he advises leaders to move on by forgiving them just as they expect Allah (SWT) to forgive them. The rationality offered here is that God has given one a position like that explained in the earlier chapter, where verse number 43: 32 is quoted from the Holy Quran:

> *We have apportioned among them their livelihood in the life of the world, and raised some of them above others in rank that some of them take labour from others.* (Quran 43: 32)

Hence the rank and status is raised by God to whom even the leader is answerable (refer to law of accountability in Islam in Chapter 2).

In another saying in *NahjulBalagha* (English translation available under the title "Peak of Eloquence"), Imam Ali wrote to his governor in Azerbaijan:

> Your job is not a juicy morsel provided to you. It is only a trust committed to your care. You have been appointed by your superior a shepherd (to look after the flock of people placed under you). As such you have no right to deal with the people in a despotic manner. (see *Nahjul Balagha*, Letter 5)

Imam Ali rules out the autocratic style of leadership when dealing with those placed under one's command. The clear justification is explained in a further saying, No. 112, where Imam Ali clarifies:

> No leader is superior to Divine Guidance.

Through this final chapter, we are weaving pieces together though the law of accountability and the belief in Allah (SWT). The leader's actions and behavior are expected to be moral and ethical in treating the subordinates, making decisions, delegating tasks, and carrying any mission forward. Islamic leadership principles are well-defined and the fact that public and private lives are not separate entities in the Islamic belief system, imply that, if anything, Islamic leadership principles are based on morality as explained in the belief system.

Islamic leaders are required to be thoughtful, empathetic, and compassionate and loving leaders; the expected outcome of this behavior is that leaders would then be fair and just.

In the corporate world today, where fresh scandals are uncovered every now and then, there is an evident crisis as seen in organizational leadership; moral leadership is the savior. However, the western/contemporary school gets stuck into deciding what is right and wrong, permissible or not, legal or otherwise, and who decides. The set of moral principles used is developed by a sound conscience; the question remains, what is a sound conscience? From the Islamic perspective, this is straightforwardly achievable. The law of permissibility defines the allowable actions; hence Islamic leadership principles are grounded in morality as defined in the religious premise. Also recall from Chapter 1 that, business aims in the Islamic lens are not to do with profit maximization and therefore Islamic leadership is not concerned about reporting to stakeholders on delivering the best results in terms of numbers; it is all about the ability to look at oneself in the mirror and being able to tell oneself that as a leader he or she has accomplished the right thing.

Learning Check: Be Sure You Can

- Explain Imam Ali's call of a loving leader and his understanding to kinds of human beings.
- Understand in what context Islam does not approve of the autocratic leadership style.

Study Question

How can you relate moral leadership from the western school of thought to leadership as explained from the Islamic perspective?

Summary

In the premise of this chapter, we have looked at Islamic leadership principles. We began by emphasizing through a saying of Imam Ali, that leadership is very much an art and therefore can be taught and learned. We then extracted principles from the holy prophet's character and behavior, which like his sayings and his religion are comprehensive and all-sided. We took stock of these as guidelines because the Holy Quran, the book of Allah (SWT), defined him as an example to follow. As he possessed the necessary qualities of leadership, we have extracted some of these within the text as follows:

Morality in actions as an example from the life of the holy prophet (pbuh) even before he announced prophethood, pointing toward the fact that good conduct and high morals are at the heart of Islamic leadership principles.

The inspirational principles of leadership from the life of the holy prophet (pbuh) can be summarized as follows:

- Leaders need to be approachable, thoughtful, kind, tolerant, and forgiving.
- Leaders ought to be consultative, and during consultations in a multicultural environment must embrace diversity.
- Leaders must lead by example and need to display proactive interest in any assigned undertaking.
- Leaders must exercise a combination of strategic and visionary skills, where being a strategic leader implies one is focused toward envisioning a future, considering the present set of affairs and in parallel paying attention to short-term stability. A combination of visionary leadership skills implies a leader with an understanding of what is to be achieved in the long term.
- Leaders must be simplistic in their communications.
- Leaders must be considerate to the weakest among the subordinates (this weakness may be physical, old age, or any learning special needs workers may require).
- Leaders must encourage education in workers and they continuously strive to learn themselves.
- Leaders must be compassionate when dealing with their followers or workers.
- Leaders must lead an orderly and disciplined life.
- Leaders must possess perseverance and willpower.
- Leaders must be able to delegate.
- A true charismatic leader from the Islamic perspective is one with an excellent conduct.

The holy prophet emphasized the importance of leadership and he used to say: "If three persons of you travel together, choose one of you as your leader and commander."

Discussion Questions

1. List down five principles of Islamic leadership and compare these with the western school of thought.
2. If leadership can be learned, then what are the two most important steps that form the initial part of learning leadership from an Islamic perspective?
3. What are the characteristics of true charismatic leadership in Islam?

Suggestions for Further Reading

1. Abbasi, A. S., Rehman, K. U., & Abbasi, O. H. (2010). Role of Islamic leadership in value based corporate management: The case of Pakistan. *African Journal of Business Management 4*(18), 4003–4020.
2. Ali, A. J., & Weir, D. (2005). *Islamic perspectives on management and organization.*
3. Safi, L. (1995). Leadership and subordination: An Islamic perspective. *The American Journal of Islamic Social Science 12*(2).

Appendix

The Holy Quran, Surah Al-'Ahzab [verse 21]
The Holy Quran, Surah Ale Imran [verse 159]
The Holy Quran, Surah Al-Nisa' [verse 124]
The Holy Quran, Surah al-Ra'd [verse 11]
The Holy Quran, Surah Al-Zukhruf [verse 32]
The Holy Quran, Surah Az-Zukhruf [verse 32]
The Holy Quran, Surah Al-Baqarah [verse 282]
The Holy Quran, Surah Al-'Isra' [verse 34]
The Holy Quran, Surah Al-'Isra' [verse 35]
The Holy Quran, Surah Al-Jumu'ah [verse 10]
The Holy Quran, Surah Al-Jumu'ah [verse 9]
The Holy Quran, Surah Al-Jumu'ah [verse 11]
The Holy Quran, Surah Al-Zumar [verse 9]
The Holy Quran, Surah an-Nahl [verse 91]
The Holy Quran, Surah An-Nisa' [verse 135]
The Holy Quran, Surah As-Saff [verse 2-3]
The Holy Quran, Surah Al Imran [verse 122]
The Holy Quran, Surah Al Imran [verse 159]
The Holy Quran, Surah Al-A'araf [verse 10]
The Holy Quran, Surah alA'raf, [verse 31]
The Holy Quran, Surah alA'raf, [verse 32]
The Holy Quran, Surah al-Baqarah [verse 222]
The Holy Quran, Surah al-Baqarah, [verse 172]
The Holy Quran, Surah Al-'Isra' [verse 35]
The Holy Quran, Surah al-Muddath-thir [verse 38]
The Holy Quran, Surat Al-Baqarah [verse 275]
The Holy Quran, Surat 'Ali 'Imran [verse 31]
The Holy Quran, Surat An-Nahl [verse 12]
The Holy Quran, Surat An-Najm [verses 3-4]
The Holy Quran, Surat At-Talaq [verse 2-3]

Notes

Some Opening Pointers

1. Lewis (2005).
2. Ash-Shaykh-ut-Tusi (1390 AH), p. 324.
3. Imam Sadiq was the sixth descendant from the lineage of the holy prophet Muhammad (pbuh).
4. Majlisi (1982), p. 5.
5. Kulayni (1978).

Chapter 1

1. Chong and Liu (2009).
2. Blanchard (2012).
3. Saeed, Ahmed, and Mukhtar (2001).
4. Uddin (2003).
5. Part of 2011 Census, Key Statistics for Local Authorities in England and Wales Release (2011).
6. Kamel and Pawan (2010).
7. Kazmi (2007).

Chapter 2

1. Velasquez (2005), p. 5.
2. Salih (research); Hikmah 161.
3. Majlisi (1982), p. 135, hadith # 71.
4. Conroy and Emerson (2004).
5. Abuznaid (2009).
6. Nizam, Aldossary, and Ibrahmin (2012).
7. Edward (2006).
8. Al-Jibouri (2013).
9. Majlisi (1982), p. 96.
10. Danley, Harrick, Strickland, and Sullivan (1991).
11. Steiner and Gilliland (1996).
12. Ash-Shaykh-us-Saduq (1403 AH), p. 286.
13. Ash-Shaykh-us-Saduq (1403 AH).

Chapter 3

1. Khoei (1978), p. 13.
2. Seyedinia (2010).
3. Wilson and Liu (2010).
4. Ibn Taymiyah (1982).
5. Kim (1990).
6. Rowley (1998).
7. Ailawadi, Harlam, Cesar, and Trounce (2006).
8. Ibn al-Ukhuwwah (1983).
9. Marketing News (2008).

Chapter 4

1. Bratton and Gold (2003).
2. Tayeb (1997).
3. Parboteeah, Paik, and Cullen (2009).
4. Ali (2010).
5. Bearwell, Holden, and Claydon (2004).
6. Drucker (1954).
7. Stewart (1996).
8. Blau (1993).
9. Spector (1982).
10. Martin, Thomas, Charles, Epitropaki, and McNamara (2005).
11. Al-Jibouri (2013).
12. Abdul-Rauf (1984).
13. Majma'ul Bayan (n.d.), p. 64.
14. Group of Translators (2005).
15. Kulaini (1978).
16. Majlisi (1982).

Chapter 5

1. Avolio and Yammarino (2002).
2. Bass (1999).
3. Burns (1978).
4. Hunt and Conger (1999).
5. Kriger and Seng (2005).
6. (A.S): Stands for Alayhis Saalam meaning salutations be unto him, a traditional way of addressing holy beings in Islam.

7. Moghaddam and Gholamzadeh (2011).
8. Aabed (2006).
9. Reported by Abu Said al Khudri in Abu Daud, 2: 721, Chapter 933, hadith #2602.
10. NahjulBalagha (73rd saying).
11. Allison, Eylon, Beggan, and Bachelder (2009).
12. Heifetz (1994).
13. Ciulla (1995).
14. Sankar (2003).
15. Haykal and Muhammad (1976).
16. Kulaini (1978).
17. Leadership and Change (2012).
18. Baumeister and Tierney (2011).
19. Karp (2012).

References

Aabed, A. (2006). *A study of Islamic leadership theory and practice in K-12 Islamic schools in Michigan.* (Doctoral dissertation), Brigham Young University.

Abdul-Rauf, M. (1984). *A Muslim's Reflection on Democratic Capitalism.* Washington, DC: American Enterprise Institute for Public Policy Research.

Abuznaid, S. A. (2009). Business ethics in Islam: The glaring gap in practice. *International Journal of Islamic and Middle Eastern Finance and Management 2*(4), 278–288.

Ailawadi, K. L., Harlam, B. A., Cesar, J., & Trounce, D. (2006). Promotion profitability for a retailer: the role of promotion, brand, category, and store characteristics. *Journal of Marketing Research 43*(4), 518–535.

Ali, A. J. (2010). Islamic challenges to HR in modern organizations. *Personnel Review 39*(6), 692–711.

Al-Jibouri, Y. (2013). *Nahjul-Balagha: Path of Eloquence* (Vol. 2). Bloomington: Authorhouse.

Allison, S. T., Eylon, D., Beggan, J. K., & Bachelder, J. (2009). The demise of leadership: Positivity and negativity biases in evaluations of dead leaders. *The Leadership Quarterly 20*(2), 115–129.

Ash-Shaykh-us-Saduq. (1403 AH). *Al-Khisal.* Qum, Iran: Mu'assisat-un-Nashr-ul-Islami.

Ash-Shaykh-ut-Tusi. (1390 AH). *At-Tahthib.* Tehran, Dar-ul-Kutub-il Islamiyyah.

Avolio, B. J., & Yammarino, F. J. (2002). *Transformational and Charismatic Leadership: The Road Ahead.* Mahwah, NJ: Erlbaum.

Bass, B. M. (1998). *Transformational Leadership: Industrial, Military and Educational Impact.* Mahwah, NJ: Erlbaum.

Baumeister, R., & Tierney, J. (2011). *Willpower. Rediscovering the Greatest Human Strength.* New York, NY: The Penguin Press.

Beardwell, I., Holden, L., & Claydon, T. (2004). *Human Resource Management a Contemporary Approach* (4th ed.). Harlow: Prentice Hall.

Blanchard, M. C. (2012). *Saudi Arabia: Background and U.S. Relations. CRS Report for Congress* (7-5700). Retrieved June 8, 2013, from Congressional Research Service http://www.fas.org/sgp/crs/mideast/RL33533.pdf

Bratton, J., & Gold, J. (2003). *Human Resource Management: Theory and Practice* (3rd ed.). Hampshire: Palgrave Macmillan.

Burns, J. M. (1978). *Leadership.* New York, NY: Harper and Row.

Chong, B. S., & Liu, M-H. (2009). Islamic banking: Interest-free or interest based? *Pacific-Basin Finance Journal 17*(1), 125–144.

Ciulla, B. J. (1995). Leadership ethics: Mapping the territory. *Business Ethics Quarterly 5*(1), 5–28.

Conroy, S. J., & Emerson, T. L. N. (2004). Business ethics and religion: Religiosity as a predictor of ethical awareness among students. *Journal of Business Ethics 50*, 383–396.

Danley, J., Harrick, E., Strickland, D., & Sullivan, G. (1991). HR ethical situations: *Human Resources Management 26*, 1–12.

Drucker, P. (1954). *The Practice of Management.* New York, NY: Harper.

Edward, R. (2006). *The Enron Scandal: The Crime, Scandal, Tragedy, and Controversy of the Century.* Retrieved June 2012, from http://voices.yahoo.com/the-enron-scandal-crime-scandal-tragedy-controversy-136695.html

Group of Translators. (2005). *A Brief History of the Fourteen Infallibles.* Iran: Ansariyan Publications.

Haykal, M. H., & Muhammad, H. (1935[1976]). In I. M. El Faruqi (Trans.), *The Life of Muhammad.* Cairo, Egypt: American Trust Publishers.

Heifetz, R. A. (1994). *Leadership Without Easy Answers.* Cambridge, MA: Harvard University Press.

Hunt, J. G., & Conger, J. A. (1999). From where we sit: An assessment of transformational and charismatic leadership research. *Leadership Quarterly 10*(3), 335–343.

Ibn al-Ukhuwwah, Diya' al-Din Muhammad. (1983). In R. Levy (Trans.), *Ma'alim al-Qurbah fi Ahkam al-Hisbah.* London: MESSRS Luzak.

Kamel, M., & Pawan, S. B. (2010). Introduction: Islam and human resource management. *Personnel Review 39*(6), 685.

Karp, T. (2012). A Lack of Willpower May Influence a Leader's Ability to Act Morally. *The Journal of Values-Based Leadership 5*(2), Article 9. Retrieved from http://scholar.valpo.edu/jvbl/vol5/iss2/9

Kazmi, A. (2007, May). *Managing from Islamic Perspectives: Some Preliminary Findings from Malaysian Muslim-Managed Organizations.* Paper presented at the International Conference on Management from Islamic Perspective, Hilton Kuala Lumpur, Malaysia.

Khoei, S. A. (1978). *Rationality of Islam.* Pakistan: Islamic Seminary Publications.

Kim, P. (1990). A perspective on brands. *Journal of Consumer Marketing 7*(4), 63–67.

Kriger, M., & Seng, Y. (2005). Leadership with inner meaning: A contingency theory of leadership based on the worldviews of five religions. *The Leadership Quarterly 16*(5), 771–806.

Kulaini, M. I. Y. (1978). *Kafi* (Vol. 1, hadith # 1). California: Khurasan Islamic Research Centre.

Kulaini, M. I. Y. (1978). *Kafi* (Vol. 5, p. 84). California: Khurasan Islamic Research Centre.

Kulaini, M. I. Y. (1978). *Kafi* (Vol. 8, p. 230). California: Khurasan Islamic Research Centre.

Leadership and Change. (2012). *The rise of the compassionate leader: Should you be cruel to be kind?* Knowledge@Australian School of Business.

Lewis, M. K. (2005). Islamic corporate governance. *Review of Islamic Economics 9*(1), 5–29.

Majlisi, M. B. (1982). *Biharul-Anwar [Oceans of Light]* (Vol. 103, p. 5). Beirut, Al vafa institute. Retrieved July 29, 2013, from www.mezan.net/books/behar.html

Majlisi, M. B. (1982). *Biharul-Anwar [Oceans of Light]* (Vol. 15, p. 135, hadith # 71). Beirut, Al vafa institute. Retrieved July 29, 2013, from www.mezan.net/books/behar.html

Majlisi, M. B. (1982). *Biharul-Anwar [Oceans of Light]* (Vol. 2, p. 28). Beirut, Al vafa institute. Retrieved July 29, 2013, from www.mezan.net/books/behar.html

Marketing News. (2008). Marketing defined. *Marketing News, 42*, pp. 28–29.

Martin, R., Thomas, G., Charles, C., Epitropaki, O., & McNamara, R. (2005). The role of leader member exchanges in mediating the relationship between locus of control & work reactions. *Journal of Organisational & Occupational Psychology 78*, 141–147.

Moghaddam, M., & Gholamzadeh, M. (2011). Discourse analysis of Nahjul Balagha (Peak of Eloquence) statements: Reacting to some social issues. *International Journal of Business and Social Science 2*(24), 168–173.

Nizam, M., Aldossary, A. A., & Ibrahim, J. (2012). Ethical communication in IT project from an Islamic perspective. *World of Computer Science and Information Technology Journal 2*(4), 142–146.

Parboteeah, K. P., Paik, Y., & Cullen, J. B. (2009). Religious groups and work values a focus on Buddhism, Christianity, Hinduism, and Islam. *International Journal of Cross Cultural Management 9*(1), 51–67.

Part of 2011 Census, Key Statistics for Local Authorities in England and Wales Release. (2011). *Religion in England and Wales 2011*. Retrieved May 15, 2013, from Office for National Statistics: http://www.ons.gov.uk/ons/rel/census/2011-census/key-statistics-for-local-authorities-in-england-and-wales/rpt-religion.html

Rowley, J. (1998). Promotion and marketing communications in the information marketplace. *Library Review 47*(8), 383–387.

Saeed, M., Ahmed, Z. U., & Mukhtar, S. (2001). International marketing ethics from an Islamic perspective: A value-maximization approach. *Journal of Business Ethics 32*, 127–142.

Imam Talib, A. (n.d.). Hikmah . In Salih, S. (Ed.), *Nahjul Balaghah* (161). Cairo, Egypt: Nashre Dar Al-Hijrah.

Sankar, Y. (2003). Character not charisma is the critical measure of leadership excellence. *Journal of Leadership and Organizational Studies 9*(4), 45–55.

Seyedinia, S. A. (2010). Consumption and consumerism from the viewpoint of Islam and economic sociology. *A Quarterly Journal in Islamic Economics Eghtesad-e-Islami 9*(34).

Steiner, D. D., & Gilliland, S. W. (1996). Fairness reactions to personnel selection techniques in France and the United States. *Journal of Applied Psychology 81*(2), 134–141.

Stewart, T. A. (1996, May 13). Human resources bites back. *Fortune*, 175.

Tayeb, M. H. (1997). Islamic revival in Asia and human resource management. *Employee relations 17*(4), 352–364.

Uddin, S. J. (2003). Understanding the Framework of Business in Islam in an Era of Globalization: A Review, Business Ethics. *A European Review 12*(1).

Velasquez, M. G. (2005). *Business ethics, a teaching and learning classroom edition: Concepts and cases.* (6th ed.). Prentice Hall.

Wilson, J. A. J., & Liu, J. (2010). Shaping the Halal into a brand? *Journal of Islamic Marketing 1*(2),107–123.

Index

Adl (justice), 21–22
Allah (SWT), xvii–xviii, xxii, 17–19, 50, 59, 83
Alternative ethical systems, 11–12

Business ethics
    accords in Islam, 24–25
    alternative ethical systems, 11–12
    Islamic ethical system, 11–12
    law of permissibility, 13–14
    vs. legislation, 14–15
    moral standards, 13–14
    partnerships, 26
    prayer timings and business dealings, 23–24
    weighing, 25

Charismatic leadership, 92–93
Consumerism, 33
Contemporary management, 5, 7, 55

Decision making
    ethical perspectives, 49
    human resources, 27–28
    purchase and sales, 28

Ethical dilemmas, 26–28
Ethical marketing
    definition, 47
    and Islamic marketing, 50
    perspectives, 48
    selective, 50–51

Hadith, xviii, 11, 14, 17, 28
Halal business, 14
Holy Prophet (pbuh), 71–72, 83–87, 97
Holy Quran, xvii–xviii, xix–xxii, 23–26
honesty, 19–21
HRM. *See* Human resource management

Human resource management (HRM)
    definition, 56
    implications
        belief system, 60–61
        locus of control factor, 58–60
        managerial, 61
    influence and teachings of Islam, 56–57
    knowledge acquisition
        attainment, 73
        dispersion process, 74
        Islamic and western perspectives, 75–76
        praising the Lord, 73–74
        in western schools, 74–75
    management hierarchy
        knowledge acquisition, 70–72
        progress of worker, 69–70
        responsibility, 67–68
        self-progress, 67–68
        social situation, 65–66
        work settings progress, 66–67
    rules and practices, 62–64

Islam
    commercial activity, xxii–xxiv
    definition, xvii
    intention role, xxiii–xxiv
    prayers and prayers for sustenance, xxi–xxii
    responsibility for human beings, xviii–xix
    trade importance, xix–xxi
Islamic business ethics (IBE)
    definition, 15
    law sources, 16
    oxymoron, 16
    reasons for studying, 15–16
Islamic ethical system
    vs. alternative ethical systems, 11–12
    honesty, 19–21
    justice, 21–22

INDEX

Taqwa, 19
Tawakkal, 17–19
Islamic finance. *See* Islamic management (IM) principles
Islamic human resource management. *See* Human resource management (HRM)
Islamic law sources, xvii–xviii
Islamic leader delegates, 91–92
Islamic legislation *vs.* business ethics, 14–15
Islamic management (IM) principles
  globalization, 5
  muslim customers, 4
  for readers, 5–7
  staggering growth, 4–5
  western/contemporary management schools, 7
Islamic marketing
  branding, 42–43
  consumption model, 34
  and ethical marketing, 50
  permissible business delivering allowable products, 34–35
  pricing, 41–42
  production and product, 35–36
  product quality, 40
  promotion strategies, 43–46
Islamic model of consumption, 34
Islamic product development process
  need refinement, 38
  principle, 37–38
  vertical growth, 38
Islamic system of practice, xvii

justice, 21–22

Knowledge acquisition
  attainment, 73
  dispersion process, 74
  Islamic and western perspectives, 75–76
  management hierarchy, 70–72
  praising the Lord, 73–74
  in western schools, 74–75

Law of permissibility, 13–14
Leadership
  charismatic, 92–93
  consistency, 90–91
  education, 88–89
  Imman Ali advices, 93–96
  inspirational principles, 97
  Islamic delegates, 91–92
  Islamic perspectives, 81–83
  life of Holy Prophet, 83–87
  loyal and passionate, 89–90
  orderliness, 90–91
  perseverance, 91

Marketing, 51. *See also* Ethical marketing; Islamic marketing

Oath taking, 29
Oxymoron, 16

Pbuh, 71–72, 83–87, 97

Selective ethical marketing, 50–51
Self-appraisal, 68
Self-progress, 67–68
Sunnah, xvii–xviii, 23–26, 58, 74

Taqwa, 19
Tawakkal, 17–19

Usury, 29

Western management, 5, 7

OTHER TITLES IN THE INTERNATIONAL BUSINESS COLLECTION

Tamer Cavusgil, Georgia State, Michael Czinkota, Georgetown, and Gary Knight, Florida State University, Editors

- *Successful Cross-Cultural Management: A Guide for International Managers* by Parissa Haghirian
- *Inside Washington: Government Resources for International Business, Sixth Edition* by William Delphos
- *Practical Solutions to Global Business Negotiations* by Claude Cellich and Subhash Jain
- *Trade Promotion Strategies: Best Practices* by Claude Cellich and Michel Borgeon
- *As I Was Saying...Observations on International Business and Trade Policy, Exports, Education, and the Future* by Michael Czinkota
- *China: Doing Business in the Middle Kingdom* by Stuart Strother
- *Essential Concepts of Cross-Cultural Management: Building on What We All Share* by Lawrence A. Beer
- *As the World Turns...Observations on International Business and Policy, Going International and Transition* by Michael Czinkota
- *Assessing and Mitigating Business Risks in India* by Balbir Bhasin
- *The Emerging Markets of the Middle East: Strategies for Entry and Growth* by Tim Rogmans
- *Doing Business in China Getting Ready for the Asian Century* by Jane Menzies, Mona Chung, and Stuart Orr

Announcing the Business Expert Press Digital Library

Concise E-books Business Students Need for Classroom and Research

This book can also be purchased in an e-book collection by your library as
- a one-time purchase,
- that is owned forever,
- allows for simultaneous readers,
- has no restrictions on printing, and
- can be downloaded as PDFs from within the library community.

Our digital library collections are a great solution to beat the rising cost of textbooks. e-books can be loaded into their course management systems or onto student's e-book readers.

The **Business Expert Press** digital libraries are very affordable, with no obligation to buy in future years. For more information, please visit **www.businessexpertpress.com/librarians**. To set up a trial in the United States, please contact **Adam Chesler** at *adam.chesler@businessexpertpress.com* for all other regions, contact **Nicole Lee** at *nicole.lee@igroupnet.com*.

www.ingramcontent.com/pod-product-compliance
Lightning Source LLC
Chambersburg PA
CBHW060349190426
43201CB00043B/1843